LIVING
IN
BALANCE

BREAKING THE HABITS

LIVING IN BALANCE

BREAKING THE HABITS

GEORGE JAKAB & HARRY PELOQUIN

Pyramid

Living in Balance was produced by
Labyrinth Publishing S.A. Switzerland
Art direction and design by Carmen Strider
Photography by Alessandro Saragosa
Edited by Judith Brandt
Copyright © Text 1988 by George Jakab & Harry Peloquin
Copyright © Original illustrations 1988 by Labyrinth Publishing S.A.
All rights reserved
Printed in Hong Kong by Leefung Asco Printers Limited
Color separation by Studio Leonardo Fotolito s.r.l., Florence, Italy
Typsetting by Linograf, Florence, Italy
First Edition

First published in 1988 by
Pyramid
an imprint of Octopus Books
81 Fulham Road
London SW3 6RB

CONTENTS

PART III

EVENING

PART IV

AT YOUR LEISURE

INTRODUCTION

RELAX AND ENJOY

Imagine a tightrope walker suspended way up in the air on his high wire. The wire is vibrating under his feet as air currents push him in every possible direction. He is in constant movement, rapidly changing to adapt to the forces around him.

See his body, focused and alert yet deeply relaxed. Feel his senses tuned to razor sharp intensity, feel his exhilaration as he holds his own life in his hands. Each moment is full and complete; nothing is missing.

That place deep within his core that is totally still and silent and unwavering is the essence of what we mean by balance. To have great intensity and spirit available to us in every moment balanced by a deep inner relaxation and joy is what *Living in Balance* is all about.

When an experienced body therapist looks at a person he focuses on two main areas. He sees the structure of the individual's body with all its possibilities and its limitations. He also examines the functional side, that is, how the person uses the body that life has given him. It is very easy to introduce new choices into the way that we move, and these new choices can deeply and positively affect the whole quality of our lives.

The body, mind and heart are all interconnected. Affect one and you influence the others. For example, shedding excess weight improves physical health. But that is only the beginning. The whole self improves; we feel happier, brighter, sexier, more alive and alert.

Losing weight is sometimes a difficult undertaking. It is possible to change the way we move and carry ourselves, and the way we relate to ourselves and to others, with much less effort. The exercises and techniques in this book have been specifically designed to be done in a matter of minutes, during the course of the normal day. They are simple enough to do without professional supervision, at home, in the car, at the office, while shopping – even at a party. Many can be done alone, while others can be shared with a loved-one or a friend. They largely involve the body, but they also stimulate the mind and encourage emotional expression. Most of all they provide us with a

whole new range of choices that will enhance the quality of our lives.

All that the exercises require is a few minutes now and then during the course of a normal day. Although the book covers exercises as they might be done from morning till night, there is no precise order in which they should be practiced. The emphasis is on undertaking techniques that you personally find rewarding and enjoyable.

Once a technique is mastered, it's time to move on to others. The book does not encourage repetition – there is no virtue in being bored. Rather, the emphasis is on the new, especially within the context of those everyday activities which are normally done in a habitual and uninspired way – like brushing teeth, or while stuck in a traffic jam, while relating to familiar people, or dancing in a disco. For if we are able to introduce new choices, new movement, and new style into our everyday activities then they stop being everyday and become special – even magical.

One general warning. The techniques in this book have been created and adapted to be as safe

as possible. They are designed to be very simple. The keyword is to take them easily. Go gently through the movements, especially on the first try. This should be a safeguard against strain. You are not being asked to force yourself into any movement that doesn't come of its own accord. Be sure to balance out an exercise done with one side of the body by always doing it on the other side. Should one side be stiffer than the other, start with that side. If any exercise causes pain, leave it for later, or forget about it altogether. The body may not be accustomed to performing some movements and a certain amount of muscular ache may result, which is natural. But the ache should leave after a few days, and if this is not the case something is wrong.

People with severe back problems, heart trouble, or any major ailment should consult their physician before attempting some of the more vigorous exercises.

Remember. The main idea behind these techniques is to get more out of life. Relax and enjoy yourself.

OPENING EXERCISE

BETWEEN THE LINES

Suddenly she was awake! For a few moments it was impossible to remember where she was. The smells, the sounds, the very feel of the space around her – even in the darkness – were completely strange. Then, with a physical jolt, the memories of last night hit her. She sat up with a start, letting the satin sheet slide off her body. It was only when she saw her proud breasts by the dim light of dancing moonbeams that she realized she was naked. Before she had a chance to accept this, her senses received another signal which made her whole body shudder in fear – or was it delight?

Stop reading for a moment and just feel your breath. Don't change the pattern of it in any way; in fact exaggerate it a little so you can feel it more fully. Is it slightly faster than usual and moving in your upper chest? Or were you holding your breath? Don't try to figure anything out, just experience the quality of your breath for a few seconds...

Now, continue reading, and at the same time stay alert to the breath. Is it changing now as you notice it – getting slower and deeper – or does it seem to be getting more agitated? Are you finding that this exercise amuses you or is it making you a bit jittery? Maybe you want to smoke a cigarette or to change position. Just note what your body is asking for and go with it.

Scientists have recently unearthed a strange and sinister new virus, unusually sturdy, highly contagious and lethal to human beings. To avoid widespread panic, the governments involved have decided not to disclose any information as to its nature. It has been estimated that by the year 1991 one third of the world's population will have contracted the deadly disease it carries – incurably.

Breathe! Did you stop breathing? Feel the position of your head and neck at this moment. Do not change anything yet – just feel. Is your head at a comfortable angle? Is it in a restful position or is it tilted a bit forward? Feel your jaws. Are they held slightly slack or a bit clenched? What does the area around your mouth feel like? Does it have some expression or is it at rest? Now keep reading and feel your eyes. Are they wide open or slightly squinting. Or are they relaxed? Is one of your eyebrows slightly raised? Are the eyes alert and awake or do they wish to close for a moment or be rubbed gently? Does the skin on your face feel tight or slack? Take a few moments right now to touch the face with your hands and do something to it to make it feel better...

Did you do it? If not, why not? Not interested? Are you in a hurry to read on? If you did try it, was it worthwhile? Is your breathing any different now? Normally, a face that is touched caringly, by yourself or another, becomes immediately more aware of itself. That awareness leads to a relaxation which affects other parts of the body (such as respiration) as well as other functions.

Changes in the rhythm of breathing happen continually during the course of daily life. Usually we are unaware of our breath except in extreme

1 Notice the tension in the hands, elbows and arms, shoulders raised and hunched so that the neck has disappeared. The head could fall off at any moment and he's not having any fun.

2 That's better! Head has freedom of movement, eyes are relaxed, the back is supported and the hands are able to move. Reading is fun again.

situations, like after a hard exertion or in sexual excitement or intense anger.

Go to your neck and shoulders and arms and hands now. Are you holding the book in a relaxed, comfortable manner? Are your shoulders at rest or slightly held up in the air? Are the muscles of your upper arm working at all right now or doing nothing? How tightly are your fingers holding on to this book? Are they clutching it in a grip that is unnecessarily strong?

What about the position of your neck? Play with the posture of your neck for a minute to get a position that is more relaxed. Now let the shoulders drop again, and let the arms and hands be loose. Let your body move around a bit if it wants to. This little exercise is quite deceptive. Under normal circumstances, we do not pay much attention to our bodies, nor are we used to seeking out positions and postures, choices that are the most

agreeable to our physical body and its needs. And this lack of responsiveness carries over to our emotional and psychological moods and states as well.

Breathe deep and full. Feel breath and life interact within your body. Feel some of the sensations, pleasant and painful, moving through you. You can enjoy these sensations, all of them; they are signs that you are alive.

Some recent experiments in the area of human interaction have indicated very interesting findings. Researchers videotaped just a few seconds of initial interaction between two strangers. Then they replayed the video at a very slow speed so that the few seconds were shown over a number of minutes. As the two strangers began to interact, immediate changes were observed in both persons: changes in movement, posture and physical appearance; changes in the pitch, amplitude and

rhythm of the voice. The two began quite unconsciously to imitate each other in small ways, to resonate on a similar frequency. They became alike.

We have all noticed that people who spend a lot of time together acquire similar ways of thinking, often similar habits and expressions. Recent research has even shown that years spent together frequently breed identifiable physiological likenesses. But to imagine like habits and expressions all manifesting in a matter of seconds – and with strangers – is quite incredible. Personally, the closest example I'm aware of is walking tall and looking dangerous after coming out of a Clint Eastwood movie.

What we are illustrating here is this: normally, we view ourselves through fixed ideas about who we are, how we do things, etc. We imagine ourselves to be consistent, set in our ways, organized in our patterns, capable of self-discipline, reliable and stable and so on. We largely idealize these states and even hit ourselves for not coming up to scratch, even though, deep down, we dream of being as loose as the wind. There is no need to be fixed entities. The fact is we aren't – our bodies consist of ninety percent water, which makes us very fluid and flexible. Look at a baby in action and see how true this is. Still we imagine that as we grow up we are destined to become more rigid and we frequently find ourselves trapped in that image of ourselves. We build around us walls of conditioning, habit and fixed notions that serve to limit us, and we view these limitations as part of our character, our maturity. But this is rubbish. Our natural state of inner and outer balance is an ever-shifting, ever-changing affair. With a lot of help from parents, teachers and the rest we have built the walls that confine and limit us. It is therefore our freedom to choose to become more open, alive and unlimited.

One little story. A short while ago I learned to sing. I'd been dropped from music class at an early age, being told I had no ear, and had never dared sing since. My friend and I were testing a new tape deck and she challenged me to sing into it. The first half a second I was in tune and when I tried again I was in tune for five. I began to understand that my ears could actually tell me when I was out of tune, and I could get my vocal chords to follow the advice. It felt like a miracle.

What had happened? I had had this idea that I was absolutely incapable of singing. This was my reality, reinforced by others right up until this time. Suddenly a new piece of information had come along, and at that moment I was open to experimenting. My reality broadened and I haven't stop singing since.

ABOVE The choice is yours.

LEFT The natural state of inner and outer balance is an ever-shifting, ever-changing affair.

PART I

MORNING

WAKE UP

FRESH START

1 Hard to begin? Chuckle.

2 Getting into it - giggle.

3 Cracking up.

■ LAUGHTER

"Laugh and the world laughs with you; weep, and you weep alone."

In the entire world of living creatures, perhaps the most underrated gift peculiar to humankind is man's ability to laugh. Only man is sufficiently self-reflective to recognize himself in situations other than those he is actually in, and to make an ordinary event full of humor.

We mortals experience this living humor only from time to time. But it is said that certain mystics of the East have generated an immense belly-laugh on their awakening which never leaves them. Perhaps this mystical belly-laugh is one of man's highest forms of expression. Utterly unique, it comes in response to a visionary understanding, and it comes in solitude, whereas our more earthly laughter distinguishes itself from both this kind and the fixed faces of animals by being a social phenomenon. Setting joke books and TV comedies aside, we laugh in groups.

Laughter is a formidable expression of our individual energy, almost like an explosion catapulting out of our bodies and into the world we share with others. As with anything that creates an upheaval and re-settling of our body energies, it is a powerful tool for transformation.

And laughter is truly the best medicine. Modern psychologists and general practitioners have discovered that there is a connection between life-long emotional troubles and certain diseases. Resentments contained in the body and not expressed for years are said to promote the severely contracted holding that leads to all kinds of serious debilities. Laughter is the body's natural painkiller and is known to facilitate healing.

Even our creativities are nurtured through play and laughter. They relax us; they expel our usual barriers of control, they lure us beyond our limitations into the new and the mysterious. Through playfulness we are more receptive to the unexpected, more willing to explore and to experiment.

Laughter shatters fear, it disintegrates burdens, it breaks up the stiff muscular cores of our psychological hurts that have been nurtured by our seriousness and self-importance. It is an affirmation of our humanness and therefore of our life. It releases tension inwardly and outwardly; it deepens our breath, excerises our lungs and increases our circulation.

Here is a very simple exercise to cultivate this gift. Remember, it takes less muscular energy to smile than it does to frown.

First thing in the morning as soon as you begin to wake up and even before there is time to set your mind in motion about the day's activities, start laughing. You will feel a little foolish at first because usually laughter is a spontaneous activity, but if you think of it as an exercise, you needn't be put off. There will be no reason to laugh; in fact you may still be quite groggy, maybe even hungover – never mind. That in itself could be comical enough! Just begin by imitating laughter: ha ha ha, hoo hoo hoo, hee hee hee. You may start off by having to make an effort, but that's okay.

Keep laughing in this way for a few minutes. Think of it as a good way to get the blood flowing. Soon, however, your mock laughter will become contagious and you will discover yourself laughing really, probably at the absurdity of the situation.

The whole exercise needn't last more than a few minutes, and regardless of whether in the beginning you manage to genuinely laugh or not, it should be repeated each morning for at least a week.

People who have tried this zany little trick have reported wonderful responses. At first many felt foolish to be doing it. But soon they reported it becoming easier and easier. And if you have a partner with you and you both are giggling together, it can become hilarious.

■ CAT STRETCH

Everyone can picture the slow and sensual stretch of a cat – simple, graceful, and obviously satisfying. None of the tension and excitement of the hunt, nor the passion of an animal in heat, but the most ordinary of acts, imbued with a life of its own.

When first waking in the morning, feel the animal in you! This is the time when your body is rested and relaxed, but probably a bit stiff as well. Take a couple of minutes while still in bed to stretch it.

Put the minimum amount of effort into it. The idea is to lengthen and loosen the muscles rather than to contract them. Twist yourself in different directions, arch your back, and wiggle around. Slowly and luxuriously, imagine yourself to be a cat, sleek and strong, no care in the world – and put all your attention into this graceful act.

Feel your body responding with pleasure as it opens up more and more. Allow the energy to flow through you without hindrance.

You can almost hear yourself purring!

■ DREAM TALES

Some twenty percent of our sleep is spent dreaming. That's about one and a half hours per night, which in an average lifetime adds up to between four and five years; no mean time to spend lost in visualizations!

Whether we remember it or not, we, and this includes babies and animals, all dream. Dreaming seems to play an important part in our interior lives, serving to organize and file away thoughts, conscious and subconscious, which have accumulated over the day. Incomplete ideas, wishes, and remembrances of the day's events are all worked on and finished off, freeing the mind of inhibitions and preparing the area for a fresh start in the morning.

Dreams are accompanied by movements of the eyeball within its socket, called rapid eye movements, or REMs. Experiments have been made on subjects who were allowed to sleep but not to dream, so that when REMs were observed the sleeper would be disturbed and his dream cycle broken. The result was irritability, uncoordinated movements, lethargy, and general listlessness in the subjects. A sleeper who is severely deprived of dreaming for a number of days will suffer temporary hallucinations and even psychotic symptoms.

All in all, dreams are important to our lives. Whatever the level of your dream remembrance, it can be increased by the use of a simple bedside journal in which you record any dreams immediately after waking up.

It will help if last thing at night before falling asleep you tell yourself several times (a kind of self-hypnosis) that you will remember your dreams when you awake. It is good to do ten minutes of relaxation beforehand, either watching the breath or some other exercise (such as *Squeeze and Relax* in the *Evening* section), to bring yourself into a more receptive space before making the suggestion.

Then in the morning you can simply open the notebook and start recording the dreams, taking care to put in as much detail as you can remember. With practice the amount recalled increases, and you start to have more and more access to your dream life.

You can also create an understanding of your dreams by simply following their patterns. Dream images repeat themselves, sometimes in detail and sometimes on a more atmospheric level. Check to see what is on your mind; maybe the dreams will give you a clue as to what you need right now.

One theory says that if you are able to remember during a dream that you are dreaming and give yourself some signal during the dream that you have decided on while awake (such as waving your hand or looking at your feet), this experience brings you into an even deeper connection with your unconscious. All of these little tricks will help you to become more of a master of the deeper levels of your mind which you may be unaware of.

...using the bedside journal.

■ THE NEW DAY

Are you one of those who wakes up in the morning, mind whirling with ideas, filled with plans and worries? Then this is for you. Transform a time of nagging thoughts into a creative experience.

The night before, prepare a pad and pen by your bedside. In the morning (perhaps after your dream review and between your cat stretch and rising) start jotting down the thoughts turning in your head. Include in this a list of the things you think you must do, whom you must call, and places you have to go. Don't edit the thoughts. Don't exclude anything just because you think it isn't good or important enough. And if the detail isn't exactly right, or you have an idea to do something you don't want anyone else to know about, don't worry, just put them all down as quickly as possible, as they come to you.

Through this process we empty our heads of nagging thoughts that would otherwise keep craning their necks for attention throughout the day and get in the way of whatever we are actually trying to get done. If certain problems have been troubling us, solutions often pop up first thing in the morning. This is because during the night we are in close contact with our subconscious, an area where an incredible amount of information is stored. We draw on this information during sleep and can have it readily available in the morning.

With particularly difficult or troubling issues, we could try thinking of the problem last thing at night. It is like feeding a question into a computer. When bodily functions are at a minimum, as during the night, the brain computer has more power to function. First thing in the morning the answer, or at least some clues to the answer, may well be there.

Jotting down the images that arise in the morning may find us writing poetry, or drawing pictures, or singing long-forgotten songs. We are sending a message to our creative faculties to come out and play with us. Art in all forms arises initially out of a need to express ourselves. One certainly does not have to be anything of an artist to enjoy self-expression, and if the early morning in bed is not a time to put aside the inner critic and let loose a little, then when is?

■ BREATHE!

This exercise is so simple that a child can perform it without any difficulty. Adults, on the other hand, have a lot more trouble! We're talking about something every living being does, all the time, non-stop – breathing.

People living in western societies have learnt very bad habits in this natural and life-supporting activity. Some hold their breath in, trying to exhale as little as possible. Others prefer to inhale the absolute minimum, just enough air needed to remain upright. Some of us hold our chests out and stomachs in, while others tighten the throat, immobilize the rib-cage, and stiffen the lower back; we stoop and twist in every direction; we freeze our jaw muscles, contort our faces, and collapse our shoulders forwards or yank them way back. In short we will do anything to avoid breathing naturally!

Why go to all this trouble to avoid an activity which is sheer joy when performed properly? Human beings are creatures of habit. Since school teaches us the art of self-control over our wild childlike rumblings, we fall into a rut with our bodies the way we do with our thoughts, and find it hard to be flexible. Nothing works so effectively in controlling our self-expression as the harnessing of the breath. Self-control may have perfectly legitimate social uses, but it needs to be more like the clothes we dress in to go out: something we put on when necessary and take off when not needed.

For example, rather than developing a mature attitude towards sex, we use shallow inhalations to control the genital area so that it does not get stimulated by the flow of the breath. Rather than confronting and coming to terms with our anger, we control it by tightening our guts and throat, thereby pushing the anger down.

Do these ploys work? Even the majority of us – we who are fairly normal – have still lost our natural innocence to some degree. Nor have we gained as much maturity as we might along the way, for one of the primary aspects of maturity is a resourcefulness that permits a number of different responses in any given situation. Control is a way of limiting our choices so that our reactions become predictable.

Throughout the book we will keep returning to breathing, as it is one of the foundations of living

I With the inhalation the torso fills up like a balloon and expands in the front, the sides, even in the back. Some effort is needed.

2 With the exhalation there is only relaxation and letting go of the air. No effort.

1 "Well, here goes..."

2 She has gently let her knees fall to the side which makes rolling onto her side easy and natural.

3 As her feet swing down the left arm gently pushes the whole torso up into sitting.

in balance. This exercise will not radically alter your breathing patterns, but will act more as an introduction to being aware of the breath. If even sometimes we come to breathe in a new way, then when we fall into our worst patterns of breathing, it will become noticeable by contrast.

To visualize the breath, just think of your torso as a balloon – it expands in every direction. On the in-breath it is being blown up. To release, one lets go of the neck of the balloon and gravity does the rest – the air rushes out by itself! The total picture is that of a continuous wave, with one step effortlessly leading to the next.

First thing in the morning, before the plans of the day have had a chance to occupy your mind, lie comfortably on your back or curled up on your side.

Begin just by noticing your breath, without any effort to change it.

Then become aware of your whole torso, from the bottom of your pelvis up to your neck, includ-

ing the front, the back and the sides. Even consider the inside of your armpits as part of the balloon.

Now gradually let your breathing fill up this balloon. No need to strain, or take a deep inhalation, just a small effort is needed on the in-breath. No effort needed at all on the out-breath.

Many people try to push the air out, thereby tightening just at the time when they should be relaxing. If tension and relaxation are equal, we are in balance.

It may take a little while to get it the first few times you experiment with this technique. But soon it will come more and more easily. Go on doing it for just five minutes every morning, and the quality of your breathing will be improved. This will also effect the results of most of the other exercises you do in this book.

A further addition is to take a few moments occasionally during the course of the day to check in

4 A moment's rest. Note that she has ended up in a straight yet relaxed position.

5 She falls forward until the weight is over her legs which are beginning to straighten and push her upward.

6 Starting the day in a new way.

on your breathing. Whenever you remember, just feel the breath for a few seconds, adjust it to the balloon-like breath, and then forget about it. This is a great way to keep relating back to yourself and to give your private self a bit of extra attention. When we are in touch with ourselves, there is always more joy and freedom in our lives.

■ ARISING

We have all heard of the guy who got out on the wrong side of the bed – he was rude and bad tempered that day – but what we may not have realized is how much truth there is in this expression. For the way in which we get out of bed does have a marked affect on the quality of the whole day to follow. There actually are better and worse ways to do it.

Here is an ideal way. Instead of sitting straight up – which is going directly against gravity and takes the most effort and muscular contraction –

simply roll onto your side first. Pull your legs a little closer to your chest. Let your feet hang off the bed. Then let the legs follow. As the legs swing down, an effortless movement that uses the force of gravity to help rather than hinder will cause the upper half of the body naturally, and with minimal energy, to swing upwards.

Breathe! Breath is the way to expand and open the body. Many people hold their breath while doing a simple thing like getting up.

Your arms are only being used to steady you; they are not needed to push you up. The arms and the shoulders stay loose and relaxed.

The momentum gained from swinging legs down and torso up can then be carried on into standing. Allow the torso to swing forwards till the weight is on top of the legs and then use the legs, designed for such activity, to propel you upwards in one smooth and flowing motion of effortless ease. This is a good reminder that life does not have to be a struggle!

THE SECRETS

INTRODUCTION

Woven into the fabric of this book are special sections which consist of the secrets of living in balance. Like all the great secrets of life, they are simple yet important truths, the kind of statements that when heard, resonate somewhere with our own understanding of life.

In order to improve the quality of life anywhere around us we need to start with the individual. A lively, relaxed and free person influences those around him by his very presence. As we grow and mature within ourselves, we affect our surroundings without even trying; it is just an organic process that mushrooms as we transform. These secrets are offered in the hope that one day soon they will not be secrets at all, but common sense lived by all.

FIRST SECRET

STARTING FROM WHERE YOU ARE

Every skier understands the importance of choosing the right slope to match his or her abilities. If the slope is too easy, skiing loses its excitement. If, on the other hand, it is too difficult, the outcome could be a broken leg. So the wise skier begins with a slope that he will be able to master quite easily yet that remains interesting enough to test his skills. Once that first run is mastered, the skier is in a position to reassess his abilities. Bearing in mind the particular conditions he faces, he chooses other runs providing different degrees of challenge.

As in skiing, so with the exercises in this book – and so with life in general. Begin by choosing exercises that attract you and that you are sure you will be able to do. All that this requires is an open and honest mind: something that sounds simple but may not be.

Many of us have been taught to put a lot of effort into developing a self-image that may, by fixed nature, not amount to what we really are at all. This is because we are actually a great deal more than what we might imagine.

Frequently by trying to fit with what is broadly

Imagine an educational system which takes into account each child's individual physical, mental, emotional, and psychological differences and weaves them into the pattern of teaching they will receive. Now look back and consider your own school.

Society has contrived to support those that support it, at the expense of the rest, leaving no room for true creativity. Competition is cut-throat, curriculums are fixed and so on. In order to take control, society – depending on the times – encourages certain human traits and suppresses others. No wonder we are all afraid to look too closely at ourselves.

But we needn't be. The truth is that as soon as we begin to look and honestly assess where we stand, we begin to reclaim our own power. Living in balance means discovering that power and making use of it in a constructive way that helps the whole being find fulfillment and equilibrium in its day-to-day life.

How we fulfill ourselves is a personal and individual affair: a rosebush fulfills itself in the scent of the rose blossom, a walnut tree does so in offering an abundance of tasty walnuts. When the groundwork is laid and the roots have sunk deep into the earth, you will have started by knowing where you are. And knowing where you are, where you stand, is the first step towards living in balance and coming into your own.

Practically speaking when doing these exercises, start with those that immediately appeal to you and are within your limits. They are mostly very simple, but different exercises suit different people. That way, not only will you not be bored, but you won't be put off if the exercise does not work for you immediately. Just experiment and see what happens! A successfully completed exercise will give you the confidence and motivation to do the more challenging ones. Soon, as more and more choices become available to you, you will be doing things that you would not have imagined possible!

speaking someone else's idea of who we should be, a great gap grows between our innate natural power and the manufactured personality we adopt as a mask. This is something that has happened to all of us to greater or lesser degrees. On an obvious level, for example, society decides that we shall wear clothes – and a certain kind for men, another kind for women. Via our education, upbringing, and all the civilizing influences of our culture they form a thick foundation to our conscious world which frequently acts as a barrier to more simple primitive energies.

IN THE BATHROOM

PRIVATE PLAYGROUND

■ TWO-WAY TOOTHBRUSHING

A moment of truth. It is early morning, just you alone in the bathroom – perhaps a rare opportunity. Who knows what lies ahead? The joys and sorrows of the coming day.

Who knows and who cares, for here and now in the bathroom, you reign. And the moment has come to embark upon a grand adventure into the unknown. It is time to brush your teeth!

Certainly if you wish you can go about it in the same way you have always done: mechanically doing a few dutiful passes. But what a way to set the tone for the day!

Instead, let's experiment. Here's a good warm-up. Stand tall in front of that mirror, take a couple of full deep breaths, and give a royal lion's roar. This roar is produced by sticking your head far forwards, lifting your eyebrows and bulging your eyes out as much as possible, and ripping out a roar just as loud as circumstances permit.

This roar will immediately bring your energy into the body and into the present moment. It awakens the slumbering beast within. If it strikes you as being pretty funny, it's perfectly permissible to laugh. Usually we take ourselves too seriously, and a good laugh at nothing in particular miraculously puts things back into perspective.

The lion's roar is only one of many good starters. Whinnying and snorting and prancing around like a horse is also fun. Indeed, any and all animal imitations are creative and get the energy moving.

Animals are at home in their bodies. Little do they care about the stock market or the laundry. They don't suffer from anorexia or obesity (unless their hormones have been messed about with). Have you ever seen an overweight sparrow? We can learn a lot about living in balance from our animal friends.

When brushing at night you will want to do more relaxing, soothing, and unwinding types of things along with it. Massaging your scalp and temples a bit or rubbing your hands together vigorously till they get warm and then placing them over your eyes are very pleasurable. Whatever you dream up is good. All we are talking about here is a few moments of your time spent focused on yourself.

We mostly move so fast we forget what we are running after. In the pursuit of a flashier job, a higher income, or a larger flock of brainy kids, we have forgotten the knack of looking within and connecting with our individual selves.

At first glance, these little exercises may appear childish – in a way they are. It is our childlike delight in the simple things in life that we have temporarily misplaced.

Now let's get back to our teeth! Actually brushing is much more than a simple act of necessary drudgery. It is a cleansing and a way of touching and relating to one of the most sensitive areas of your body.

Use a toothbrush that's not too chewed up and just the right amount of a tasty toothpaste. Don't

1 The face moves, the hand stays still... the world is upside down.

2 Let the head balance on the neck rather than holding it in place.

3 Still practicing! (left hand brush)

LEFT Funny faces make you laugh and wake you up.

be in a hurry. Slip into all the small spaces and crevices. Be sensual; be imaginative; don't be shy. Experiment with different speeds and rhythms and types of movements. Feel the immediate effect. The inside of your mouth, the gums, palate, tongue, and teeth feel more healthy and alive after a good brush.

If you notice, the hand, the whole arm... indeed the entire body are all involved in the process of brushing your teeth. Normal unconscious brushing contracts large numbers of muscles unnecessarily. This wastes energy and reinforces tension. Feel the muscles in your neck as you go. Most likely they are tightening to resist the pressure of the brush. Let the neck muscles relax. Allow the head to move back and sit loosely on top of the neck so that it is balanced on top rather than being held there. There are no anatomical reasons to hold the head in place.

Now see if your shoulders are held up in the air and jammed into your neck. Let them fall out-

wards and downwards. At first, it won't be easy: you will forget and habit will pull the shoulders up again. Don't worry, who is to know?

Pay attention to your jaw muscles too; they are tight on just about everybody. Wiggle and shake your mouth about, and rub with the knuckles as hard as you can. You will be surprised to feel your breath deepen and little waves of energy move through your body.

In the game of baseball a switch hitter is one who can swing the bat and hit the ball with either arm leading – a definite advantage. If you have any doubts that brushing your teeth without awareness creates strain, then try brushing with the opposite hand. Immediately you will notice that you are using a lot of muscles that you never imagined.

Brushing with the other hand is an exciting experience because you have to learn it anew; it cannot be done by the unpracticed arm automatically. The best way to learn is to consciously brush with

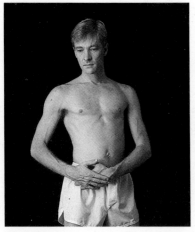 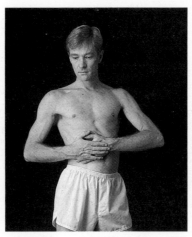 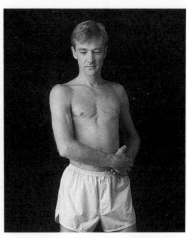

Don't be afraid to go in deep sometimes and explore your insides with your fingers. Go slow and it's impossible to hurt yourself.

the arm you normally use and then imitate the movement with the learning arm.

Several interesting things happen in the process. The teaching side learns through its teaching more relaxed and probably more efficient ways to use the arm. The learning side picks up a new skill. Furthermore, the brain is stimulated in a fresh way and called upon to function beyond its usual limits.

■ TOILET TRAINING

Improper functioning of the intestines leads to a wide range of maladies such as colitis, constipation, hemorrhoids, and cancer of the colon. Un-eliminated waste matter that sits in the colon for a long period of time can become toxic and begin to poison the whole body, giving rise to feelings of sluggishness and achyness.

But even if your colon is functioning well, there is no harm in tuning into this area more often. The Japanese refer to this area as the *hara* and consider it the center of primal energy and of a balanced connection to the earth. Those who are centered in their *hara* are characterized by courage, stamina, confidence, and strength – much like what westerners mean when they say someone is gutsy or has guts.

Normally we relate to our intestines in a limited number of ways. Westeners spend millions of dollars a year on laxatives, preferring to lubricate the intestinal channel rather than encourage it to flex its muscles more efficiently. We perform exercises to shorten the belly muscles to give the flat-bellied look; the laziest amongst us notch our belts tighter or hoist on thicker girdles. We are concerned with the way it looks from the outside, expecting that with the help of artificial products it will continue to function, and less concerned with the actual workings of the organism.

There are two simple techniques which assist the bowels in eliminating waste and at the same

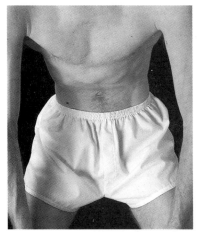

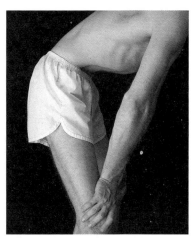

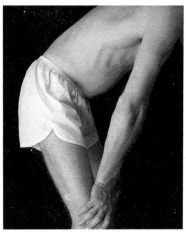

1 Pull in the muscles of the stomach and guts.

2 Very quickly – all the way in.

3 Out, in, out, in, like a tuning fork.

time help you to get in touch with this important internal organ.

■ BELLY MASSAGE

While sitting on the toilet in the morning or at any time – massage the lower part of your belly below the navel where your large intestine sits. This is done with clockwise movements, following the route that the food actually takes in traveling through our bodies. As you do this you will discover the places where there is tightness, bloating, or gas. You will feel the pockets where waste matter is lodged. Through the massage you will be able to actually move this material and help it on its way out.

■ UDIAMA

The second exercise works well only on an empty stomach. The ideal time for it is early in the morn-ing. It can be done sitting on the toilet, or standing, with knees bent and hands placed in a relaxed manner on the knees.

Begin by taking a breath in and then exhaling as fully as possible. Once the lungs are empty, slowly pull in the muscles of the stomach and guts, almost – but not quite – as far as they will go. Then, very quickly pull the muscles all the way in... then slightly out, then in and out. This sets up a vibration, like a tuning fork.

Keep going until you need to take a breath, then relax, breathing normally for a few moments. Again exhale deeply, and repeat.

The whole exercise will only take three or four minutes. It is great as a simple exercise for the belly muscles; if you are concerned about flab around that area this will tone it up. It is also ideal for increasing the blood supply there. Most important as far as the body function goes, it is wonderful for stimulating the contraction and expansion of the colon muscles which create the pumping action

needed to rid the body of waste. Finally, by bringing our awareness to our *hara*, this helps us feel more grounded and more energetic.

After a couple of weeks of doing this exercise every morning you will be much more aware of the muscles in your stomach. You will then be able to isolate and move certain specific muscles more than others.

Concentrate on moving the muscles on the right side of your body first. This is where the ascending colon is. Then follow the movement of the waste matter as it travels across from right to left in the transverse colon and then down the left side where the descending colon is. This way you are actually assisting the waste matter on its journey out of the body.

In order to command one muscle area to move and then another next to it, we have to focus our minds on the job. Once the mind and body are working together on it, our basic intimacy with that area increases – we have learned a new way of doing something.

■ MIRROR GAZING

We include this in the morning section, though for you the right time could be whenever you have five unhurried minutes between changing clothes and are not feeling too self-critical.

Stand naked in front of a mirror (full length is the best). Close your eyes and begin to feel your breath, allowing it to get a little deeper than normal.

Start swinging and moving your body very gently, letting the movement be relaxed and sensual. Feel your body from the inside enjoying the life that courses through it.

All the mystics agree that at the deepest levels the greatest joy arises from simply being alive and in the present moment, wanting and needing nothing. Just celebrating the miraculous fact of our existence is the state that we are tuning into in this exercise.

We have all had moments – gazing at a sweeping landscape, playing with a newborn baby – when we simply enjoy what we are doing without evaluating it in any way. This capacity brings us to a sense of peace and harmony. All we need do is set aside the part of us that constantly wants to sum up and move on and step back inside ourselves.

Being able to look at yourself with an unconditional acceptance leads to a capacity to nurture yourself which then carries over into the rest of your life.

Here you are standing in front of the mirror, swaying with closed eyes. You are about to look in a relaxed way at something that you normally appraise the most – your own body. Just before you open your eyes make an agreement with yourself to look uncritically. There is a way of look-ing which is just looking: not at the blemishes, not even at what you consider to be your good points – just looking.

Open your eyes; keep swaying and moving and breathing. Keep your gaze slightly un-focused as you look at yourself. You might feel uncomfortable looking in this way, and thoughts and comments will interfere. Take no notice of them! Keep your attention with the movement of the body and in the gaze. You have given yourself five minutes, remember! Don't be in a hurry to reject your own mirror-image.

If the frolicking of a kitten can make you wonder at the miracle of life, just look at your own body. Watching that you don't zero in on any particular part, consider how harmoniously your body functions, and view its reflection with the same awe with which you gaze on the cat.

If your mind is so strong that it comes up with more of the same old comments, then just see if

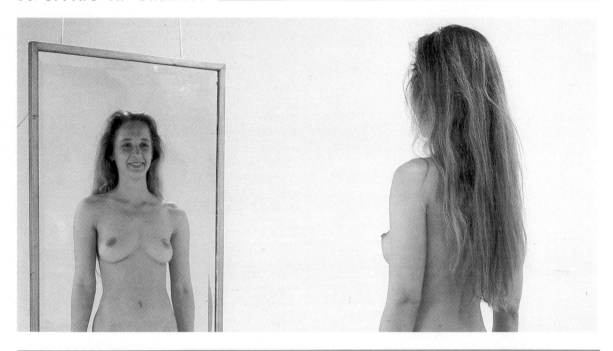

you can change the emphasis. Each time it criticizes, meet what it says, and then move on to something you feel differently about: "Yes, I can see that the nose is big. Fine, so I have a big nose. But look at those eyes, the color of the iris, the slant of the brows, the curve of the cheekbones, etc." Do not fight with a strong critical faculty because that will only give it more power. Just change criticism to simple dispassionate noting, and as the mind relaxes, go back to looking. When it comes in again, then switch over to noting what it is saying without getting caught up in any one point.

Your mind is not deliberately trying to sabotage you. It has just been over-trained in a certain way to the exclusion of other parts. It is not used to being left out of the picture, and it gets jumpy at being excluded. Explain to yourself that it is just a technique you are doing for a few minutes. You will call on it again when you need its services.

Try this exercise for a few minutes a day for a few weeks and you'll find a new way of relating to your body. A capacity to be non-judgmental will reach into the rest of your life and you'll enjoy ordinary things more wholeheartedly. Even your critical faculties, now getting a rest, will be more discriminating when called into action.

Finally, consider this: have you ever gazed on a natural landscape and thought, "That lake would look better over to the east more; those trees are a bit too green and too far forward..."? Probably not. We look at nature appreciating it as it is. However, looking at your own back garden you will probably want to move the odd bush or pathway to suit your tastes. The difference is identification.

We identify with what is ours and judge it differently – and that is only natural. Where it gets compulsive is when we are constantly wanting things to be different. For then we never give ourselves the chance to simply enjoy things as they are and just relax and commune with nature.

WANTING THE BODY YOU'VE ALWAYS HAD

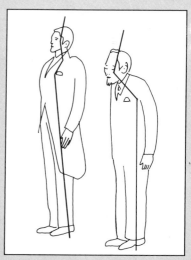

THE AMERICAN WAY
Notice how Ronald Regan holds his power in his upper chest and shoulders.

THE JAPANESE WAY
The Japanese man's strenght is in his *hara* which is below the navel.

Not satisfied with your body? No one is! Even the most adored and glamorous men and women in the world judge themselves and always find imperfections. Finding imperfections prevents

Live in the right age and the right place and you too can have a body like these. But be careful – make sure your choice is right or the cost could be too high.

us from totally enjoying our bodies and using them to the fullest. We are engaged in an internal war to get things just right: lose weight, add more muscle, get a nose job, etc. It is an endless process of trying to fix things, a bitter resignation leading to a poor self-image, or a denial of the body altogether.

When Harry was eighteen, his passions were wrestling and weight lifting and he was the proud owner of a very muscular body. He went to a body-work therapist for a session one day who pointed out all of the structural flaws, saying that the very muscles he loved were an armoring against really feeling the world. Harry was shattered, of course, and his whole self-image changed in a matter of an hour.

The idea of the perfect body is the ultimate myth. Yet the fact is that we have been taught to judge ourselves mercilessly. The cosmetics industry, the plastic surgeons and trend-makers of all kinds would suffer great losses if we didn't. The harder we are on ourselves the better it is for business.

This is not suggesting that we shouldn't have critical faculties. It is always healthy and fun to be looking good. The trouble is we have become obsessed with self-critical values. Thousands of eight and nine-year old kids who show no evidence of weight problems whatever are reportedly getting into serious dieting.

Since views of what is attractive or sexy are constantly changing anyway, even if we do achieve a certain look, by the time we've got it, it's out of style.

After World War II, when scarcity was at an end, it became fashionable to be plump and rounded like Marylin Monroe or John Wayne. But in the anti-materialistic years that followed during the sixties, the skinny appearances of Twiggy and Jimi Hendrix were in. By the eighties we had moved toward the sleek and powerful look of a Grace Jones or Sylvester Stallone.

Heredity and environmental influences create a variety of needs and aspirations among all of us, for sure. But there are different body types and we are all unique. Even identical twins are only similar at first glance.

A pamphlet came in the mail not long ago advertising a body-building course: "Now you too can have the body you've always wanted," it said. We dreamed up an alternative pamphlet that we headed: "Now you too can want the body you've always had."

This change of focus radically alters the whole affair. We are what we are what we are, and this is the point from which we begin our journey. Imperfection allows us to grow and mature through the constant flux of being an evolving organism. We are all special in our own way. If we can simply accept ourselves as we are right now, and come to love ourselves, the more beauty will shine out, whether body-perfect or not.

When we love ourselves we function out of love. We do what is right for us, not because we wish to stand out in a crowd, but because it feels good to do so.

Change your focus. When you look in the mirror don't just notice the faults; use what you like about yourself as your groundwork. Don't just be aware of the aches and tight places; feel the parts that are in good order. This is not to say we should ignore the pains, but just that we do not make that our emphasis. Try saying to yourself, "Yes, my neck is hurting and it must be telling me something. But my legs are full of energy, maybe I'll let them dance a bit. I bet it will loosen my neck as well."

Loving ourselves just as we are is a simple thing, though strangely it is not something we are encouraged to feel as we are growing up. Competition constantly invites comparison that inevitably leads to self-criticism. We are taught to love our neighbor – whomever he is – but not ourselves.

Start with yourself. Start right now to love your body the way it is. Soon you will find yourself living in balance.

Live in the wrong age and the wrong place and you too could have a body like these. And still it might cost you a fortune.

IN THE SHOWER

SLIPPING AND SLIDING

■ SINGING

The morning shower is a time of great creativity. With the good acoustics, it's an immediate invitation to experiment with all forms of song.

Whether your preference is for rock, folk or opera, let loose and really sing your heart out.

Singing is good for the circulation, for the vocal chords, for loosening the muscles in the neck and shoulders, and for the lungs. It is great for the head too, taking it away from our worries and troubles and bringing it into a time when nothing bothers us – the present. Music is guaranteed to lift our spirits out of any hole and help us fly.

From time to time, try listening to your song. Don't worry if you can't remember the words – make them up, or talk gibberish. Just fala-lala-la will do. Listening to your singing as you shower will also help you hear the actual tonal quality of your voice as others hear it. But that is secondary. For the sake of your own body, a full volume of uplifting song will do the trick, regardless of whether you think you can sing or not! Complaining neighbors? Tell them you've fallen in love!

■ SOAPING WITH LOVE

Singing is not the only technique possible in the shower. As you soap yourself imagine your body as a child's body, or perhaps the body of your lover, you are touching. When we touch a loved one we do so with great care and respect but rarely do we pay such a tribute to our own bodies. They serve us magnificently in an enormous variety of ways, and who better to appreciate this wondrous thing than you yourself?

As you apply the soap, slow down, and become more and more aware of where your hand is going, and which part of your body is becoming soft at any given moment. Doing this thing you've done daily for your whole life, it's hard not to be mechanical and let your mind wander. But bring your thoughts back each time to the thing in hand. Remember, there is almost no other time that two areas of your own nerve endings are in continuous contact.

There are many ways you can celebrate your body. Be curious about it. Allow the contact of your hand on the skin and the sensuous feel of the slippery soap to soothe you. Explore all the nooks and crannies and crevices. The human body is unrivaled in the world as a work of art. Treat is as such.

Now see if you can include a bit of self-massage in the soaping. Create novel ways of getting to those hard-to-reach areas. Do a few bends and stretches.

Touching our bodies with love is a concept which may strike us as unusual. We tend to take our bodies for granted and to treat them as if they were tools somehow separate from ourselves, to be hoisted and manipulated. Normally, if we twist an ankle and have to hobble to the bus stop we feel angry with our foot for not operating when needed. But why be divided against a part of your own self?

The stimulating effects of alternating hot and cold water can be as invigorating as a Scandinavian sauna.

Giving our bodies the care we would give our lover's body frequently invites slightly squeamish thoughts. Yet think of all the amazing things our bodies do for us. And for sure being able to love ourselves makes it easier for us to love and be loved by others.

■ HOT AND COLD
Feeling sluggish and bad tempered and having trouble waking up? Here's a shocker! After your usual hot shower, quickly turn on the cold water full blast. Too devastating a thought? Then try cool.

Shout, and jump around to absorb the shock. And keep breathing – short and quick if you have to. Give yourself thirty seconds to two minutes, then turn to warm. Each time you repeat the exercise it will be less of a shock and more of an invigorating massage. The largest sensory area of your body will be tingling all over.

Under hot water the pores open and under the cold they close. In winter when it's near to freezing, it's good to finish with a cold shower to keep the heat in. Do the reverse when the weather's hot.

Not only is the skin stimulated, but the internal organs also get a dose from this exercise. Some people swear by it for chronic headaches as well. It's wonderful for poor blood circulation, gets the corpuscles racing around the arteries, and helps if you have a tendency to get the chills during the day or do a job that involves a lot of standing and is giving you trouble with your legs.

The sauna is a more sophisticated form of this routine, and the Scandinavians, who have been practicing it for decades, claim it keeps away colds and gives you a long and active life. Don't be shy to make brrrr sounds as the chill hits your skin. Do it with a sense of humor and you can have a lot of fun – especially if there's someone you love to enjoy it with you!

▪ SHAKING ALL OVER

When the shower's over rather than reaching immediately for your towel, shake your body to get the water off. This is how all animals do it and it is an invigorating, energizing activity. Shake arms and legs and torso separately and use your hands as well to brush the water off.

When you do eventually use the towel, be sure to rub quite vigorously. This activity really opens the pores, removes dead skin and stimulates the blood circulation. The whole activity brings you more fully alive in your body, moving the last vestiges of sleep and making you prepared to meet the day with enthusiasm.

Soaping in the shower can help transform mechanical activities into a loving massage.

Give your body a good shake. Like a polar bear after a swim.

CREATIVE MISTAKE-MAKING

Columbus made a mistake and wasted a lot of time doing it. He thought he had reached India, but all he did was discover a whole new world! Alexander Flemming made a mistake: he forgot to throw away a dish of bacteria he was cultivating. When he returned from being away on a trip he discovered that the air-borne mold that had settled on the bacteria had killed it. Penicillin was the result! One of our forefathers dug up a brown root and, finding it un-eatable, made the mistake of tossing it into the fire. The smell it produced got the taste buds going, and the baked potato became staple diet!

We are a cautious species; we don't like to make mistakes. We would rather do things in the old familiar way even though it becomes boring and mechanical because doing what we know to work

gets us through our routines – it may even be more efficient. Yet repeating things over and over frequently involves a major sacrifice – the magic of exploration.

Exploration, search and discovery are natural human drives. That we feel the need to explore far-off places for three weeks of each year is testament to that urge. Just as the manner in which we do it – with package tours and pre-planned sightseeing – is testament to our fear. We like to choose but we like to limit our choices. One of the reasons seems to be that modern life and the consumer society make simple exploration impossible – or so it appears – because they have deprived us of the necessity to explore and experiment with the small things of life in our day-to-day world. Never taking risks or being willing to make mistakes in little

Futura

provocative
adventurous
contemporary

FOOD FOR THOUGHT BOOKSHOP
Via della Terme di Caracalla
00100 Rome

☎ 5797 . 3127

things, we get out of practice for the big ones. But if we do take risks and are willing to make mistakes, we become explorers of our daily lives and stop craving for the big moment when we can take off for a safari and perhaps bump into a giraffe.

Become an explorer at home, and you will see. And start small. Begin by making the kinds of mistakes that are not going to lead to a flooded cellar or a garage door that won't shut. And if routine, at first, feels far too safe to stray from then start really small: just reach for a different brand of coffee in the supermarket than your regular, and find out it doesn't actually tear your tongue off. You may even prefer it. This might seem to be the most trivial beginning to breaking the ice of your routine, but we do need to start from where we are, and sometimes it's those small things that limber us up to making exploration and change our very way of life.

Now try taking the wrong way home, or leave the car at the edge of the nearest park and walk to work. Experiment with a new eating place for lunch – or go for a completely new recipe for your next dinner gathering.

All these may end up being mistakes, but not with lasting effects. And besides, a new way of doing something, if it doesn't actually replace the old, will always add a little something to it and to you. At the very least it will highlight the virtues of the old way. And you will discover the joy of being creative for the sake of it.

Now move on to new trivia. Here's a little trick for rearranging your room: take a small mirror, preferably a wide-angled one like the wing mirror of a car, and walk around looking only through the mirror. You'll be surprised at how different it seems. Normally we arrange our room and leave it at that. This is a device to see it freshly as if it were someone else's room. It's exactly the same but the mirror-image will reveal all sorts of gaps, messes, or misplaced pieces of furniture. Now rearrange it. Take the time, get the kids to help, and have fun with it.

Now try making a bigger mistake! Dream up something you've always wanted to do but never dared. With these little experiments behind you, you'll have no difficulty.

Learning doesn't need to stop in childhood, which is when we normally imagine all mistakes to come to an end. Through experiment and mistake, through trial and error, we learn the mundane lessons and the sacred lessons at the same time; through our entire lives we evolve and mature mainly by exploring the new.

And what is new for someone else may not be new for you. If you always play safe, then play sorry for a change. But if you are a compulsive table-hopper, someone who's always checking if the grass ain't greener, try taking the risk of being bored by doing what you've always done before, in a new way perhaps.

The mistakes in themselves don't really teach us anything, of course. Where they help us is in our own willingness to learn from them. Noticing what happens when we make them, not with embarrassment or denial but with simple curiosity and the courage to tolerate our fear, we come to understand our own limitations as an individual. One wise friend once said that the only difference between the courageous and the timid is not that the timid feel afraid and the courageous don't, but that the courageous go ahead despite their fear. We all feel fear, of course. Understanding our own limitations, coupled with the courage to experiment each time slightly beyond their boundaries, is the key to successful mistake-making.

Once we've learned whatever it is we must learn, we will stop making the same mistake over and over. No need to beat ourselves because we should have known better. Beating ourselves is one way we mis-channel energy from the art of learning from our mistakes. Just assume that once you've burned your hands on one stove you won't need to burn them again on another one. You'll be alert and save your hands for cooking fine foods instead.

PART II
DAYTIME

■ SIMPLY SITTING

Meditation is one of the most powerful tools we have at our disposal for living in balance. Unfortunately most people associate meditation with arduous practices, with ascetic yogis in remote mountain caves and with arcane rituals under the moonlight. Certainly difficult techniques do exist, yet they by no means share a monopoly on meditation. It is a process that is available to all, in any situation – and more necessary than ever before.

To be in meditation is to be in the present moment. It is a state where the ever-busy mind has stopped its incessant activity; no more worrying, planning or plotting, nor dreaming. It is a mind simply at rest (sometimes known as no-mind).

An intricate and valuable tool, is the mind – capable of things we still barely have an inkling of. But it does tend to be a nag! The notion that we should keep our mind operating even when it isn't actually needed is rather like advocating moving your legs up and down even after you have climbed off the bicycle. Meditation closes down the mind for a while and gives it a rest, which then opens the way for us to experience life more directly, whether it be in nature, in relationship to others, or in experiencing ourselves. It helps us achieve a clarity which focuses our mental processes at those moments when they are needed.

Another way of saying it, is that meditation is a state of delight in one's own being. One very important point to be understood is that meditation is not something that can be done as such. One can set the scene for it, but to do it is a contradiction since it is actually a state of non-doing. You are simply at rest, alert to everything that is happening. In the same way that one can sometimes sit in the middle of a crowded, noisy room, aware of what is going on but still be relaxed and quite unaffected by it; meditation takes us one step further inside ourselves, to watching what is going on in the mind, in the body and with the feelings, without reacting to them.

However, though there may be no way to do meditation directly, there are certainly many techniques which can put you into a situation where meditation occurs. It is the technique, not the state of meditation itself, that may require some effort.

In a sense, all the exercises presented in this book can be viewed as meditation techniques. For as we experiment with new ways of doing familiar things, we become more alert to our actions and in the present moment because when faced with something new we always pay closer attention to what is going on.

The specific meditation technique that we are about to introduce you to is, paradoxically, the most simple and the most difficult of all. It can be done at any time of the day, though early in the morning, after a cup of tea or coffee, is a preferred time because we are relaxed from sleep without too many of the day's worries on our minds. Buddhist meditators claim that four a.m. is the best time, but for most of us that is a bit too drastic. If the morning is not a good time for you, find another that suits you.

Sit cross-legged or kneel on a cushion with your back as straight as possible. If you can't manage that, sit in a firm chair, but your back should be straight yet relaxed. The posture is important only in that it is conducive to sitting quite still, at ease and yet alert. When the spine is straight, our bodies are in balance with the least amount of effort needed to stay upright.

Now close your eyes and observe your breath as it moves in and out in an area just below the ribs. That's all you have to do: just watch the breath come and go, in and out, paying close attention to the simple rise and fall of the diaphragm, letting the breath move by itself without you pushing it out or sucking it in.

Of course thoughts will come and start demanding attention. Your mind will tell stories, make plans, have dialogues with people, ask for a drink, and all that. Now you will find that you are

A mind simply at rest.

about the breath. Each time, just come back to the movement of your belly.

After a while the moments when you can observe the breath without any effort will get longer and the thoughts less and less frequent. This will vary of course both during the hour that you are sitting and from one sitting to the next, depending on what is going on in your life and how many things you have on your mind. Don't be disheartened. Watching the gaps between the thoughts is meditation.

The mind feels uncomfortable when it has nothing to do. It always wants to use the time to think things out, and to fret and fantasize and create a disturbance, which is what makes this apparently simple technique so hard.

It might help to start by checking out how rarely a problem can be solved by thinking about it: actually only a tiny fraction of your thoughts not directly connected to action, operate in a creative way and alter the direction of your life. This may be hard to believe at first, but as you practice this exercise it will become more and more obvious how much time is spent brooding and inventing, without results.

no longer watching the breath but rather some movie running inside your head, probably all broken up and repeating itself. This is perfectly normal. Each time you catch yourself in it, go back to watching the breath. Your attention will wander again and again and you will keep forgetting all

Your mind will create bodily distractions too – that itch that just has to be scratched, that leg muscle that must be shifted. If possible just notice these irritations and pay no attention to them. If you really must scratch, then do so – this is not an

endurance test. But the best way is to just be a witness to what is going on and repeatedly return to the breath. Eventually there comes a point when the mind has played out all its games and gets bored with itself; then it simply shuts down. At that moment you are totally in the present.

Occasionally a pain may arise in the body. As long as it is not serious enough to signal danger, keep your posture. Don't fight or ignore the pain, but do the reverse. Stay with your relaxed breathing but focus your attention on the feeling, accepting it not as pain but as an energy. Breathe into it as if you were somehow entering it, keep on focusing, and you will find yourself diffusing it from the inside, releasing a kind of heat. This may not be successful the first few times, but as you go deeper within yourself with practice, these things will become easier and easier.

Meditating may appear to slow you down at first. But as your activities take on a more focused quality, you'll find the reverse happening: that although you may appear to be slowing down, your actions are so much more economical that you will in fact be achieving more. Everyday events that create tension in you will stop disturbing you – waiting for a bus will become a sheer pleasure! And your activities – whether it is sweeping the floor or talking to a client – will become more conscious and vital. This is the essence of a meditative life.

The ideal amount of time to be spent on this meditation is between forty-five and sixty minutes, although when you first start, you may wish to begin with a shorter length of time and work your way up. It is best to decide in advance how long you're going to sit for, even if it's only ten minutes, and to make a point of sticking to your schedule. Sometimes playing a piece of meditation music that lasts as long as you intend to sit can smooth your way.

In the beginning, when you've not yet felt the benefits, you'll need to make an effort and be really patient with yourself. But as the feel of it

ABOVE Why keep moving the legs after you've climbed off the bicycle?

LEFT There is no way to "do" meditation, but certain situations can help it happen.

starts to permeate your being it will be possible for you to take short meditation breaks during the course of your day – on the bus, at your desk, even at a party. You will be able to close your eyes for a minute or two, relax back inside, and emerge moments later, comfortable and refreshed. In time, even stopping to close your eyes will no longer be necessary. Breathing is something you are always doing, and focusing on this activity can actually be done along with all your usual daily activities without disturbing them. In fact, it will enhance them! The toughest of all is to do it while you're interacting with other people. If you can achieve that, consider yourself a meditator!

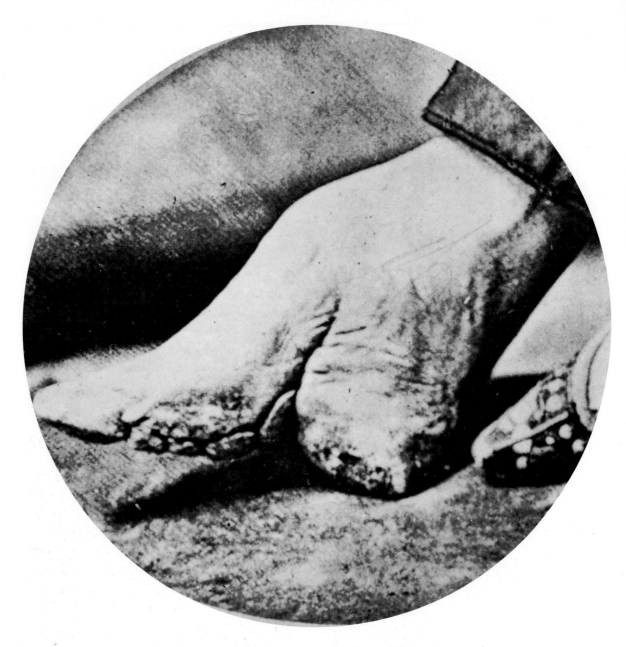

ABOVE Small is beautiful – barbaric?

RIGHT Fashions of the times.

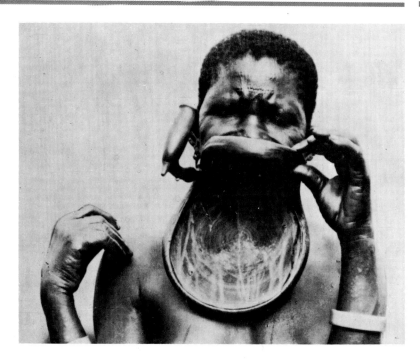

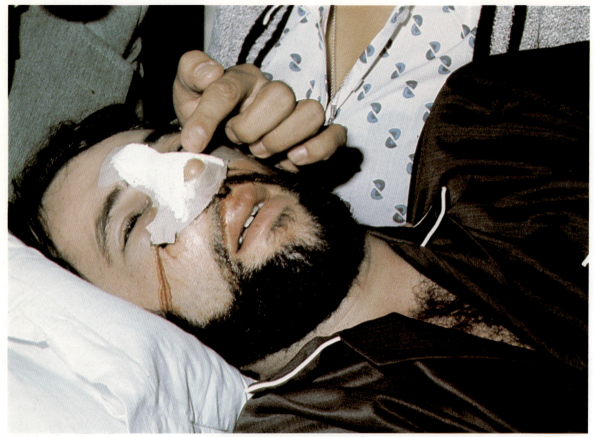

ABOVE This is civilized?   **RIGHT** Tight belts, skinny skirts and very high heels act as a straight jacket.

■ EASY DRESS

We all like clothes even when they drive us mad. We are forever discarding yesterday's favorite, buying new things, searching for the perfect combination of fashion and comfort, constantly reassessing our sartorial image and meanwhile hanging on to what grandma knitted, thinking we'll wear it one day. We experience clothes as an extension of our bodies, replacing the body in the social world as the personal packaging in which we present the product of our person. How we are assessed at first meeting, whether people want to employ us or lay us or simply duck, largely depends on what we wear.

Let's wear clothes we look good in, for sure. This is how we develop the individual style that forms our self-image. It's healthy and fun to take care of how we dress.

The trouble is fashion forgets people and frequently entices us to cut the legs to fit the pants. Our impressionable minds are constantly going after stuff that basically discourages comfort.

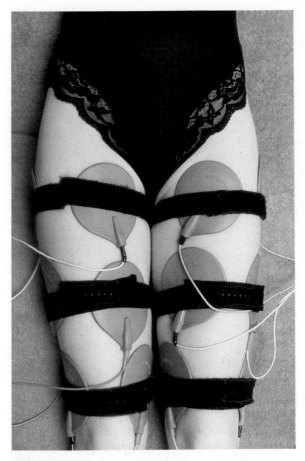

ABOVE Creating the "perfect body" can be painful.

RIGHT Dress so your body can move and breathe freely.

There's nothing new about that. A hundred years ago women were locked in corsets as tight as the rib-cage itself; they could barely breathe, and they were swathed in so many layers of silk, satin and petticoats that fainting became almost as stylish as the dresses themselves. In China, when small feet were beautiful, female babies had their feet bound from birth to inhibit growth – something we now consider barbaric. Yet look at the tortures working women today are obliged to undergo in high heels simply because they flatter the leg.

There's no need to suffer in the name of fashion. There are enough clothes that promote ease of movement which are also very stylish. The current trend for running shoes and sportswear is a healthy one, though you don't have to look as if you are on a permanent jog to be comfortable. As you get closer to your inner world, taking responsibility for yourself will probably involve examining the clothes you normally use and give you the courage to explore different styles and materials.

Here are examples of a few clothes to avoid; here also are the reasons why. Anything that is too tight restricts our outer movement, as well as the circulation and digestive processes. Trousers and pants too pinched around the waist with belts notched too far over cut the body in half and give us the feeling of being separate from our lower body. Ill-fitting shoes and high-heels make it hard to walk, and make us un-grounded as well as overworking the leg muscles and generally throwing the spine off balance. For some people, synthetic fibers irritate the skin and cause rashes, whereas natural materials allow the skin to breathe. Materials that are too heavy drag us down.

When you buy new clothes and footwear, don't just look at it in the store mirror: walk around, sit down, stand up, and see how they feel in movement. Clothes should not have to be worn in. Experience shows that sales talk about over-tight shoes stretching to fit the foot applies only to all-leather, and even then the time it takes for the shoe to fit the foot may not be worth the agony while the foot is having to fit the shoe.

Colors affect us in different ways and can change our moods. Be an innovator; develop styles and shades that suit your needs. You'll find you can go along with fashion perfectly well without being its slave.

TRAFFIC JAM

MAKING USE OF EVERY MOMENT

For many of us, there are long hours during the day when we are entirely alone: cleaning the house, doing the shopping, driving the lengths of the interminable freeways to get from one place to another. All the exercises that follow are for any of those times. We have focused on the traffic jam just because it is a representative situation, one most likely to produce the kinds of tensions we are all familiar with in modern life.

Whether you drive in the rush-hour suburbs of the US or through Europe's packed city-centers – we all get the chance to sit in a traffic jam. Stories abound of frustrated Italians knifing each other for a fender scrape, and Americans tail-gating up freeway ramps and taking pot shots through side windows. Everyone hates the interminable back-view of the car in front, and neither bumper stickers nor dingly-danglies provide enduring entertainment. Even the charm of the radio is blighted by one hysterical commercial after another.

Tension in a traffic jam comes from a difficulty we have adapting quickly to a new situation. One moment we are full speed ahead and focused on our destination. The next, we're stock still. The feeling that if we maneuvered our car here, or turned around and went another way, we'd be able to control the situation better only leads to greater frustration. A brief relief can come with changing lanes, only to be thwarted by seeing the cars in the lane you've just left zipping ahead of you!

Traffic jams are like the weather, they never discriminate. Businessmen or housewives, Rolls Royces or Volkswagens, they hold tight to anyone and everyone without playing favorites. Nor do they care whether you are suffering or enjoying yourself. Basically, a traffic jam just is.

But it is in the pure state of "just is" that it provides us with a perfect situation to practice creating one's own reality. The bumper-to-bumper crawl can be transformed into a mobile sensory laboratory. While others sit in the driver's seat fuming and scheming, you can become an emperor of your palace on wheels. Start by breathing deeply. And imagine turning up forty-five minutes late to an important meeting – not disheveled and wild-eyed, but relaxed and smiling!

■ SOLID SUPPORT

Those of us who don't spend their days serving hamburgers or dancing on the stage, do a whole lot of sitting. Cars, offices, dinner tables, football games – seats are everywhere with people sitting in them. As a posture sitting is relatively relaxing, but for those committed to chairs all day, tension and body pain is all too often the result. That's because seats aren't what they appear to be. Without good balance in the sitting position and adequate body support, certain muscles have to strain to hold us up. The lower back is in most danger. In terms of structural support, it is already the weakest part of the body, which means that even slight tension over long periods will translate into aches. As the lumbar vertebrae (lower back) and the cervical vertebrae (neck) tend to imitate one another, the lower back strain readily runs up the spine and into the neck. In driving this is further complicated by the demands of the road and the need to be constantly alert.

Statistical research shows that over eighty percent of people have back problems some time in their lives. Many suffer quite debilitating discomfort over long periods – sometimes years – and for a significant number, back pains persist to the grave.

What most people don't realize is that problems of the back take a long time to develop. There's no difficulty recognizing that shooting pain when the back pops while tying a shoelace! What we're not so familiar with is to what extent years of improper movement and lack of care have been undermining the body's inner strength. The final sudden move that does the damage actually is the proverbial straw on the poor camel's back.

By learning to sit, lie, stand and move well, we not only enjoy our bodies more, but we keep them healthy for much longer. Animals always move with ease and grace because trouble and strife usually pass them by, whereas mankind is full of worry, and the demands of modern life force us into unnatural patterns. This is further aggravated by shoes designed for a Gucci window display rather than living bone and nerve, clothes created by movie stars, and seats and beds built for expedience.

The first thing to check is whether you are slumping in your driver's seat. However relaxed it seems, slumping means asking our muscles to do a scaffolding job for the tilting structure of our vertebral column. The spine is not supporting the body as one whole but rather as individual vertebrae. Anyone who has ever tried the eastern method of carrying something heavy by sticking it on their heads rather than cradling it in their arms, will have felt the marked difference between the support they get when the spine is erect and when it is out of line. If the spine is not holding us up

then it is either the seat of the car or our muscles that do the job. By simply placing a firm pillow or rolled towel into the region of the lower back we give it the support that it needs.

The situation is further aggravated by our having to push on pedals with our feet, meaning that the leg is also in trouble. You may also wish to put some support under your thigh, near the knees, to get the leg in the best position.

If your car seat lacks good upholstery or makes

ABOVE Wrong posture. There is no support for lower back, upper back, head or knees. Notice her frown.

RIGHT Cushion supports lower back allowing upright posture. Neck and head supported.

you slump too much even with a cushion, try sitting on a board.

In driving, the shoulders tend to tense and ride up. Just keep remembering to let the shoulders down so that they are resting on top of the rib-cage rather than being suspended in the air.

This kind of relaxation applies just as much to typists, who do well to sit with good lower back support as high above their keyboard as possible, so

that the back is straight and the fingers can bop across the keys with the shoulders relaxed. Take care that you're not so high that your feet are dangling; they should be flat on the floor or resting on something.

If you are too slumped in the driving seat, breathing becomes difficult. We get less oxygen, which in turn leads to a groggy feeling – dangerous when behind the wheel. Position yourself in such a way that breathing is easier and fuller. No matter how comfortable, try not to stay in any one position for too long without moving. Even if the movement is slight, it still assists in loosening up the tight places and in helping circulation.

Let your head sit comfortably on top of the neck and shoulders rather than perched forwards. An average head weighs about fourteen pounds, which is a considerable weight for the neck muscles to hold continuously. When your head rests on top of your spine, it is able to balance there without effort.

Let it all out.

Certainly there are positions that are better than others for sitting. Later we will discuss the optimal position for sitting in a chair (see *How to Move*). However, it is important to experiment as much as possible with finding your own way. The very act of experimentation and paying attention to movement serves to improve it. It is much like fine-tuning a superb automobile: the more familiar one becomes with the workings of the car, the easier it is to correct any faults efficiently. The more attention we pay to the body the less chance there is of getting into bad habits and of things going wrong at a later stage.

■ MOBILE SCREAMING

How many times have you come home from a long drive, with all of life's pressures surrounding you, saying, "I just wanted to scream!"?

This is a simple but totally satisfying exercise. Sitting in your car, you are in your own private room. Go ahead, scream! No one can hear you. If they can, they haven't a clue who you are, and as soon as the traffic starts moving you'll never see them again. What better opportunity to do what you've always wanted to do?

Do it loud and long and full, and enjoy it. Screaming is great therapy. There are many folk who pay good money to do encounter groups that give them permission to expand their vocal chords this way. A traffic jam provides this for you on a plate – and not a penny spent.

The benefits of screaming are many: it is a good exercise for the vocal chords, the face and neck muscles; it releases tension, especially suppressed anger and fear; by being a primal activity, it reconnects us to our roots – to our bodies at the deepest level. A good scream comes from the guts and rises through the whole torso before it leaves the throat and mouth. Babies love to exercise their lungs this way. Tarzan signals his position as king of the jungle with an almighty yell. One of the strongest attractions of a roller-coaster ride, or the house of horrors, is that we are encouraged to

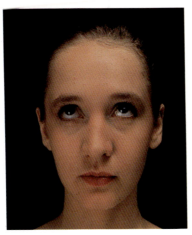

1 Place palms gently over closed eyes.

2 Open wide and roll your eyeballs.

3 Make the circles as slow and big as possible.

scream. As a form of catharsis screaming is an unparalleled cleanser and a trick to lighten up our spirits. It is a way of feeling and assessing one's own power without infringing on anyone else. Screaming deepens our breath – always therapeutic in itself, and it's terrific fun.

After any good bout of screaming you will feel refreshed and relaxed with more energy streaming through you. A natural follow-up then is to do a few physical exercises that can be done easily in the confined space of a car.

■ ROLLING EYES

Start by vigorously rubbing your hands together till the palms are hot and then gently place the palms over the eyes.

Holding your head still and keeping your jaw slack, do rotations of the eyeballs, both clockwise and counterclockwise, letting the movement be slow and the circle of the eyeball be as big as possible.

Look straight up as far as possible, then back to midpoint, and then down as far as possible. Repeat a few times and then do the same, moving the eyeballs to the sides.

Give the eyes a chance to rest in between movements and make sure you keep breathing.

Move your eyes in as many directions as possible, including going cross-eyed by looking at the tip of your nose. See how much you can move both eyes in different directions. And let the head get involved.

■ ROTATING HEAD

As you look down let the whole head go slowly down as well. Feel the back of the neck muscles get longer as your head flops forward. Then follow your eyes up till your head is tilted back and the muscles in the front of your neck are long and stretched.

The key to this exercise is elongation. Always focus your attention on the part of the neck that is

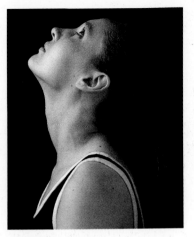

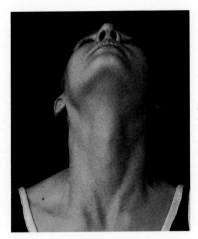

I All the way up.

2 Feel the elongation.

3 All the way down.

getting longer. Whichever direction the head is moving towards, those muscles are working by tightening and shortening. Meanwhile those on the opposite side are meant to be letting go, lengthening and stretching. Even when rotating the head in circles, there is a constant movement of muscles contracting and relaxing. If you rotate your head slowly you can feel the different muscles working.

Normally we have no difficulty in shortening and holding muscles tight. The tougher activity is to let muscles go. Here our normal habit in rotating the head would be to tighten the whole neck and all its muscle groups. This inhibits our range of motion. The word uptight describes the way we use our muscles just as vividly as what we become when we do.

The pattern that has constricted our musculature and affected our whole sense of being at ease begins to be reversed when we start placing the emphasis on letting parts go. If we were always

only to use the specific muscles needed in any one movement, it would take much less effort to move and the muscles not in use would get a chance to relax and rejuvenate themselves. One of the outcomes of most forms of exercise is to create space between muscles – untangle them so to speak – so freeing them for their separate functions.

There are many stories about the great ballet dancer, Nijinsky. Apparently he had the ability to leap so high and to come down to earth so slowly that he appeared to be defying the laws of gravity. And he himself had no explanation for this phenomenon. If we were to give an educated guess as to what was going on, it would concern the process of lengthening the body and creating space within. As any area contracts, it becomes denser and heavier. Nijinsky seemed to possess an unequaled knack of totally losing himself in the dance, and in this state everything he did was effortless even while performing arduous physical feats. It is possible that as he relaxed in the air, he

Prprprprprprr...

became lighter and more airborne, giving the appearance of slowing down his movements.

A similar grace of movement can be derived by anyone following the principles of lengthening and creating space inside.

■ HORSE LIPS

Take a deep breath and blow it out through an almost closed mouth, allowing your lips to move and vibrate with the expelling air. Horses do this frequently and a certain kind of horsy sound goes with it that you'll recognize as soon as you do it! The challenge is to relax the lips so that they really flop around. Lips and mouths are used in so many ways that the area tends to store a lot of tension. Horse lips can relieve the holding in an almost effortless way.

■ SHOULDERS TO EARS

Driving is a peculiarly twentieth-century phenomenon: sedentary concentration. Computer operators have it even worse: their heads need to stay fixed along with the rest of them. There's not much else we do that requires so little physical effort along with considerable stress. Most of the tension when driving accumulates in the poor shoulders which respond to the rigors of the road by slowly creeping up towards the ears. The longer

1 Our normal position contains so much tension that we have becomed accustomed to it.

2 Exaggerate. Touch your ears to your shoulders. Go all the way.

3 From full tension we move to its opposite, total relaxation.

your neck the further they have to creep, and the more they creep up the more the muscles have to hold them there by shortening and tightening. This causes a lot of headaches, among other things. Even if it doesn't get that far, there is still plenty of needless effort put into keeping the shoulders high (it may serve to keep your camisole strap from falling, but little else!). And when we finally leave our car, we usually manage to carry the tension with us.

Still standing in that roadblock? This exercise is basically an exaggerated series of shrugs.

Just feel the holding in your shoulder muscles for a few moments, identifying in your mind all the muscle areas involved.

Lift your shoulders and try to touch your ears with them. At the same time hold the breath in. Hold it for a good thirty seconds and then exhale, simultaneously let the arms drop. Take a couple of relaxed breaths and then repeat.

After a few times you should begin to notice some loosening. Don't worry if you feel a bit of an ache–that's a good sign and it means something is shifting. The ache will go the more frequently you do the exercise.

The theory behind this move is that consciously exaggerating and supporting the points of tension, we give them time to relax. Part of the mechanism of stress is that energy is stuck, unable to move and dissipate itself. By increasing the tension, we begin the pendulum swinging, and once movement is established the swing towards relaxation is a natural consequence. Understand this principle, and you can apply it to many things in your day-to-day life.

■ HAND MASSAGE

We use our hands so often and for such a wide range of activities, that we'd be at a loss with just one tied behind our back. Yet we give so little attention to these, most precious of tools.

With the hand massage, whatever feels right is

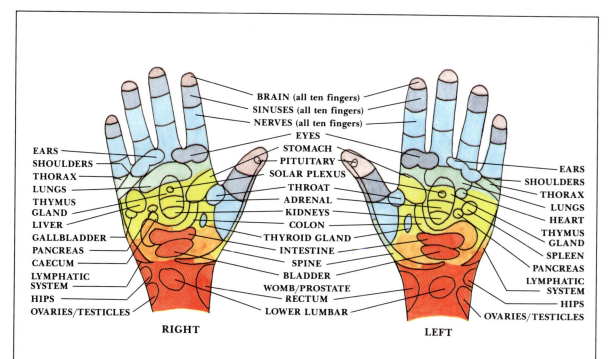

BRAIN (all ten fingers)
SINUSES (all ten fingers)
NERVES (all ten fingers)
EYES
STOMACH
PITUITARY
SOLAR PLEXUS
THROAT
ADRENAL
KIDNEYS
COLON
THYROID GLAND
INTESTINE
SPINE
BLADDER
WOMB/PROSTATE
RECTUM
LOWER LUMBAR

EARS
SHOULDERS
THORAX
LUNGS
THYMUS GLAND
LIVER
GALLBLADDER
PANCREAS
CAECUM
LYMPHATIC SYSTEM
HIPS
OVARIES/TESTICLES

RIGHT

EARS
SHOULDERS
THORAX
LUNGS
HEART
THYMUS GLAND
SPLEEN
PANCREAS
LYMPHATIC SYSTEM
HIPS
OVARIES/TESTICLES

LEFT

You can find points that relax you,
others that stimulate you. Work deep
into the points that hurt and the
corresponding parts of your body
will respond in time. You can
diagnose and help to heal yourself.

1 Twist your pelvis, turning the head as far as possible to the right.

2 And to the left.

3 Stretch out your arms and rotate the hands.

right. Stretch the fingers. Rotate gently at the joints. Move the hand with the assistance of the other hand in ways you normally don't. Bend the fingers backwards, bend the wrist back. Shake the whole hand vigorously letting the fingers flop around loosely.

Be creative. Take a jar of good cream with you in the car and rub it in, emphasizing between the joints.

Very quickly you will notice the hands relaxing. Accupressure meridians from all over the body come to the hand, so you will be working on the whole of you through pressing various points between the tiny bones of the metacarpus.

The diagram illustrates the connection between the hands and the rest of the body. As you massage deeply in the hand, some spots will hurt more than others; refer to the chart and you can see which part of the body is asking attention. By working the painful point in the hand you are stimulating the nerve pathways to the correspond-

ing organ or body part, and helping to accelerate the healing process.

If you have some problem in your body, constipation for example, check the diagram and work on healing yourself while at the wheel. While most people will be getting ill with frustration straining in the driver's seat, you'll be getting better!

■ SHORT STRETCHES

There are plenty of stretches you can try while sitting in your car.

Turn slowly from side to side, twisting your body as far as it will go in one direction, all the time breathing in a relaxed way and gently twisting a little further.

Put your arms out horizontally – left arm out through the window (you don't need a super-reach if you're right-hand drive! It's your right arm that goes out the window). Now make little circles with your arms in a clockwise and counterclockwise direction. Somebody behind you may think you're

4 Grip your hands, one over the shoulder and one behind the back. If you can't reach, hold a handkerchief and grip that instead.

5 Turn your torso one way while twisting the head and eyes in the opposite direction. Reverse the process.

6 Massage the knee, going in deeply with finger tips.

giving strange hand-signals but as long as you're both stationery, he can only scratch his head.

Put one arm behind your head, the other behind your back, and see if you can grip your fingers together. If you can't reach, take a handkerchief and grip that instead. Do it gently, keep breathing and relaxing into the shoulder and don't strain, and remember to relax totally for a few seconds afterwards. This is a great one for releasing shoulder tension.

Turn your head in one direction while turning your shoulders the opposite way.

Take your shoes off, shake your feet, wiggle your toes, rotate the ankles, and bring your toes towards the head and then down towards the ground.

Massage your knees with your hands, attempting to loosen up the whole joint.

Rock from side to side, moving from the pelvis. Arch your lower back and then curve it in the opposite direction.

Grip the steering wheel as tight as you can and then let your hands go. Repeat a few of times.

Rub your scalp and gently tug on your hair.

Create your own stretches, remembering to stay relaxed and easy with the process. Invent exercises you can continue to do while sitting in other places, like the office or in front of the TV.

Exercise does not have to be vigorous and sweaty to be effective. Although the body appreciates a good workout, even these small movements invigorate and refresh the body, keeping it loose and supple, especially if one or two are done several times a day. Anyone who has done yoga will know how beneficial even the tiniest stretches are when we take our muscles in directions normal movement doesn't.

■ FOOD FOR SENSE

The latter half of the twentieth century has seen an assault on the senses unknown in human history

7 Flexing up.

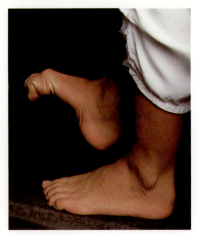

8 Flexing down.

9 Massage the scalp.

– call it the age of sensory overload. Hollywood movies spend tens of millions on their bigger and brighter special effects in an effort to dent our insatiable appetite for visual experience. Rock bands crank up the volumes of their PA systems just to force their way into our dulled ears. Every product on the supermarket shelves has its own powerful smell devised to distinguish it from the next.

The result of this constant bombardment has been to create sensory blinders that force us to focus our senses on survival alone – a necessary enough arrangement, otherwise crossing the street at a busy intersection would become too dangerous a task.

With all this sensory unsubtlety, our nerve-endings are conditioned to operate at a very superficial level. But that does not mean they are not still capable of reaching some depth. Sitting in your mobile lab you have the chance to explore the more discriminating areas of your nose, ears and fingertips.

Be sure to focus on one of the six senses at a time, and allow it to take you on a little voyage of its own. Very quickly you will notice your senses expanding, becoming richer and subtler, and it will become an everyday source of amusement and amazement.

Listen attentively to the music you enjoy – it can be a transcendental experience. Choose beforehand a mixture of your favorite tapes along with perhaps one you've never heard before, making sure you cover a range of different moods. Then, whatever feelings you wish to enhance you have right there at the push of a button.

A nibble at your favorite Swiss chocolate or savory snack can make your taste buds dance. Experiment with different flavors, always remembering quality rather than quantity, and bring along the paper napkins in case you get crumbs on your suit. Driving itself prohibits any large eating binges – luckily. Watermelon may be the juiciest but (despite the picture) you're not really expected

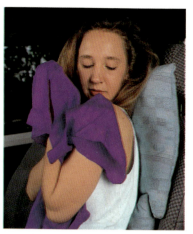

1 Something tasty. **2** Something sweet. **3** Something soft.

to cut and pip while standing still on the freeway. And the steering wheel won't like sharing your hands with sweet and sour spareribs, either. Stick to bite-sized stuff and eat it one by one, giving your tongue full range of the taste as you go.

And there are fabrics too, such as silks (a whole range of different-feeling silks from raw to satin), angora, fur, etc., for the fingers to stroke and the eyes to feast on. Try smelling them too.

There are scents, local and exotic ones, in the form of flowers, perfumes or incense, dried pot-pourri, or even wood and leather – most things have an odor we usually miss. Take at least two at a time on each trip, so they can be picked out in contrast to each other. Smells, unless they are very strong, tend to have a short life-span even for the most discerning of noses.

Now only one step remains to the exercise: to train the senses to be more and less sensitive in appropriate response to different situations. And this traffic jam can be of great help.

As you are obliged to pay attention to the cars as well as the sensory experiments, you will need to keep shifting your point of focus. From the scent of the flower to the road, to the touch of silk and back to the road again. You are training your attention to move quickly and effortlessly between two different types of activity, one of single-focused concentration and the other of general expansion. Just keep shifting your attention easily and smoothly, taking care not to get too fixed and giving priority all the time to the necessary functions of your car.

The more you practice this technique, giving as fully as possible your whole attention to one sense at a time, the more you will notice a carry-over into the rest of your life. A certain sensual wealth will follow; what is nowadays an almost defunct art of perception will suddenly be returned to you. And there'll be no danger of your ever drifting off. The demands of your car will have kept you grounded.

SET YOUR OWN STAGE

Imagine a day after a huge mid-winter snowfall. To the commuter it is a nightmare; to the skier it is paradise; to the kids it is a magical kingdom; to the man who shovels snow, another job. It's the same snow but viewed very differently through the eyes of the beholder. Each view is the individual's reality.

Humanity agrees on the reality of the need for food and shelter, yet some live in igloos, others in palaces. Tastes in food range from a vegetarian diet of rice and lentils, to the appetite for raw meat.

Can we alter and affect our realities? Why not? The Quakers and the Mormons, tired of religious persecution, packed their bags and set off to create their own lifestyle. Meanwhile countless opium addicts stay where they are while traveling on the wings of their drug-induced realities. Political and religious beliefs can become so strong that one nation or creed is forever trying to impose its version of reality on another. The more sophisticated a culture becomes, the more varied and numerous are the realities it can contain.

The question is, must we take drugs or be a millionaire in order to create our own reality?

There is no need because we are already in a position to do it. We can create our lives once we begin to take back our personal power and to assume responsibility for ourselves. Then we automatically and spontaneously begin the process. And we are in a position to do this right now: we have the tools, the know-how, in fact everything is poised at the ready. All it takes is a bit of courage to admit to ourselves that it is possible, and the willingness to experiment with our daily lives.

The preliminary is to take stock of where we are right now. As every gardener knows, we prepare the soil before we plant the seeds. Through an honest self-appraisal, free of criticism and judgment, we get in touch with where we are with ourselves.

Let's say we are serving five to ten years in prison: now there are certain restrictions imposed on us from the beginning. If our reaction is to say that we can do nothing that we want to do until we are released, then that becomes our reality. By accepting and taking responsibility for what has happened in the past to get us into the situation we are in now, we begin to take steps to create a new present situation for ourselves from which we can emerge in a fresh way. Serving time is an expression used by prisoners to describe their situation, but it could well be one many of us might use to describe areas of our lives we conduct unwillingly. We serve time at work in order to be free to go on vacation. We serve time with our colleagues, dealers and mechanics in order to be free with our husbands, wives, or children. Or vice versa, we serve time with our families in order to be free to be with our lovers, sailboats or drinking-companions. For none of us enjoy total freedom in every sense of the word, though the extent to which we inhabit personal prisons may be less obvious than it is to those in jail. We are talking here about that same freedom frequently referred to by the mystics: one that is of an inner nature, unaffected by external circumstance. It is a freedom we can all work and strive towards no matter what our external situation is. Even inside an actual prison, a man who creates his own reality is free. And even the freest and richest man can be a slave to all that happens to him.

■ PRIVATE CHATS

Whether we are aware of it or not, we all talk to ourselves. Those of us who do it aloud, risk being committed to a mental institution. The rest of us keep it inside.

Mostly the chatter creates a filter through which we interpret everything going on around us in our own private way. And the inner anxiety created by not being quite sure if we have perceived things correctly, raises our stress level considerably.

Several things can come of choosing to do this chattering consciously and deliberately. First of all, we get to see how much we do actually talk to ourselves – which comes as something of a surprise! And we discover how rarely we notice what it is we are actually saying. Once we really hear it, it no longer needs to be said again and again. Reminding yourself over and over to book that airline flight could turn into a nagging concern without the flight ever being booked. By nightfall, you're probably left merely anxious, without quite knowing what about.

Talk to yourself consciously out loud, and listen to what you are saying. You will become more efficient at filtering out the important information this way. You may even wish to take notes, which could range from memory joggers to poetry and insightful observations.

Psychologists tend to agree that we are all filled with multiple personalities – each and every one of us is a crowd. As long as there is some order in this crowd, no problem. Chaos comes when the voices start fighting amongst themselves.

As you talk consciously you will notice that the conflicting parts, when each is given a chance to say its piece, relax and leave you at peace. Some voices are more dominant than others and tend to push the less-vocal down. Listen for the submerged voices and give them a chance to speak.

For example, driving to work in the morning your businessman-self, the go-getter, is running

You are your own captive audience.

the show. But as a result, your relax-on-the-beach person finds itself repressed. Not liking to be ignored, it gets back at you by filling your mind with a beautiful beach scene, and before you know it, you've dreamed your way into the car in front of you. If your new rocketed insurance premiums eat too large a hole in your pocket, the outcome may be a cancellation of that long-deserved vacation, and the beach scene is gone for good! Now give the lazy side of you the chance to voice its mind and consciously you alter the scenario. "Of course I could do with a holiday. Just get on and enjoy the job and the holiday will follow of its own accord."

Letting the craziness within show itself actually makes us more sane.

Our concern here has been in coming to recognize what the inner chatter has to tell us, but more is said about the mind's activities in the section called *Simply Sitting*, where we talk about reducing the level of chatter altogether. Both eventually help us become masters rather than slaves of our inner voices.

■ GIBBERISH

Gibberish is a novel and effective way to relax and unwind an over-active mind. The mind operates through symbols, words and pictures, and by connecting these images it forms concepts and ideas. Sometimes, perhaps in the early morning, it is difficult to get the brain functioning quickly and effectively. At other times the brain does the reverse and gets out of hand like a computer gone wild and no cancel key!

Gibberish is said to have been first developed by a Sufi mystic called Gibber as a technique aimed at slowing down the mind. It is actually a form of meditation.

All you need do is to start talking nonsense and making meaningless sounds, as if fluently speaking a foreign language: habala go nasporita baba bulu minota ta pana. Actually, anything goes, provided it makes no sense whatsoever.

Imagine yourself to be an Italian businessman in the Galeria in Milan consulting with a colleague, or purchasing a new car at the best possible price. You are all hand gestures, facial expressions, plus a six-to-the-dozen stream of musical words. It'll feel funny to say things that make no sense, but you're alone, so who cares?

If you like, practice first by addressing yourself to a child, preferably a baby. He will greatly enjoy all the excitement and probably talk gibberish back. It works fine even with a cat. Babble till you get used to the sound of your own voice out loud. Engage in really animated conversation, using the whole body. There is no need to have a sequence or control in the speech – in fact, the more disjointed the better.

One friend, feeling a little stupid at first finding words to make up, used to speak the alphabet in a continuous stream. As if each letter were a meaningful word in itself, she would break here and there for inflection, emphasis and argument, but never actually utter a single word of sense. This even allowed her to get angry when she was feeling that way while remaining playful all the time.

In the car, give it all you've got space for. Listen to what you're saying. Soon the mind stops trying to make any sense of what is going on and the exercise goes from being a mental effort to healthy physical expression. The energy moves out of the mind and into the body.

This technique also works well at night as a cure for insomnia, or can be used before meals to finish with mind work and make ready for relaxed eating. If your room-mate or your partner has a sense of humor, do it with them. It makes a great five-minute introduction to any of the relating exercises later in this book (see the *At your Leisure* section). Whenever you choose, have a good time with it.

■ ON YOUR OWN

There are now over five billion people on the face of the earth. Being alone is quickly becoming a luxury. We are naturally social creatures, yet we all need time to ourselves, and we rarely get it because we're usually surrounded by family, work-mates, and neighbors. In fact we have become so accustomed to being with others that we are sometimes afraid to be on our own. Even when physically alone we switch on the radio or reach for the TV dial. Yet almost only alone, can we plumb our inner being to its depth and discover its versatility and originality. It is our own selves we must rely on finally for a sense of humor and for strength and meaning.

The trickiest and easiest exercise in this section is simply to allow yourself to be alone with yourself in your car.

Relax and just enjoy being alone without trying to change anything. Don't think ahead to where you're going or what you're going to do when you

What a rare treat it is to be alone these days.

get home; don't go rerunning that morning's events; just keep the tape deck off, the radio dial tuned out and check your immediate environment.

At first it will be difficult. We're so used to doing something, being active and busy. Try making a slight adjustment of attitude. Let yourself feel grateful for the chance to be by yourself with nothing to do and nowhere to go.

We have focused on the traffic jam for these exercises just because it highlights a time of enforced solitude usually combined with an acute sense of frustration. But there's no need to limit yourself to doing these exercises only in traffic. They can all actually be done any time when you are alone and want to shift your focus from a stressful situation to something more enjoyable. Once you feel comfortable doing them alone, you will find yourself able to do many of them even when others are around. What's more, your doing them might arouse curiosity: some of your office mates and family might want to try them too.

HOW TO MOVE

FROM DONALD DUCK TO NIJINSKY

If, as the saying goes, a picture is worth a thousand words, then the way we move speaks volumes about who we are and how we perceive the world as well as how well we fit into the situations of our everyday lives.

To test out this idea for yourself, stand with eyes closed in front of a mirror and picture yourself with someone that you fear. It may be your boss, your mother-in-law, or the neighborhood bully from your childhood.

Assume an attitude of fear and helplessness where your body feels tight and contracted and in a defensive pose. Now open your eyes and view yourself in the mirror for a few moments.

Close your eyes again and this time imagine that you have successfully faced up to the person you feared and are feeling strong and in the height of your power. As you are doing this let your body straighten up and assume its position of strength. Then open your eyes and look again. The difference is usually quite dramatic and helps to illustrate just two of the many pictures that we show to the world.

These movements or postures can also be called energy patterns. Each pattern presents a certain type of energy that we project to the world: fear, power, love, hate, success, failure, excitement, boredom and so on.

Each energy pattern has certain stances associated with it. If we are feeling very happy there appears an appropriate set of movements in our body. We feel and look light, and there is more spring in our step. A trained and observant eye can actually see a direction to the flow of bodily energy, which in the above examples would be upwards.

It is important to realize that by altering the way we move we can change the way we are feeling. If you walk around on purpose all slumped over, with your head bent forward, eyes looking down, dragging your feet, in no time at all you will start to feel tired and depressed.

To begin to get a feeling for energy patterns and how much movement affects the way we are, experiment with the two following moving games.

■ MOVING GAMES

Go out on a busy street and start following someone and mimicking their movements. Move at their pace, swing your arms and legs in the same way, and hold your head and shoulders as they do. Check for every detail. If you get into it, in no time at all you will feel you are the person in front of you. Busy office worker in a hurry, teen-ager checking things out – you will not only be able to tell their moods, you will actually start to feel them as your own.

I have followed Japanese people down the road and felt suddenly oriental, moving in a manner, as if from a point of focus totally centered in the *hara*.

Moving in new ways shows us new aspects of ourselves and gives us a tangible means of moving

Have fun at the next party you go to spotting all the different types of people and ther corresponding postures. Can you find: the intellectual, the artist, the hustler, the gorilla, the biker, the bible thumper, the slouch, the seductress?

from one mood to another. Just try walking tall with a bounce in your step, whistling a tune, and feeling miserable. It can't be done. Sometimes we feel low and we cannot for the life of us figure out why. Could it be that in our laziness, from within our limited choices, we have chosen to remain stuck in a depressed mood. First take responsibility for how you feel and notice your desire to change it. Then this will do the trick.

Here is a second exercise you can do in the privacy of your own room – or even at a party. Have a go at some of the following ways of moving, and get a feeling of how strongly movement affects us. They are called games – they are meant to be fun. It just depends on how fully you allow yourself to enter the spirit of the movement. The more you get into it, the more you get out of it.

Ballerina: walk on tiptoe like a ballerina, doing pirouettes and leaps. The energy is light and airy and moves up. You are connected to the sky and can almost fly.

Gorilla: imagine you are a gorilla, powerful and grounded. Sure-footed, you hop around beating your chest. Feel energy flowing into you from the earth, giving you great strength.

Stubborn Kid: pout, stamp and kick.

Tribal Walking: stomp this time, but with rhythm.

Eastern Warrior: in the east and in the martial arts, the center of one's strength is in the *hara*, located two or three inches below the navel – move from there.

Western Warrior: western strength and movement comes from the shoulders – walk like John Wayne.

T'ai Chi: move in slow motion; with every step, breathe into the earth and get grounded – be solid as a tree.

Harlem Shuffle: every part of the body moves to a beat, just for the sake of bopping around.

Movie Star: pretend to be a famous actor or actress on stage performing. Project yourself out

I Dropped my ice cream cone.

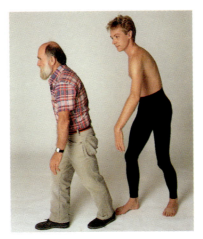

2 Keep on truckin'.

3 Get down!

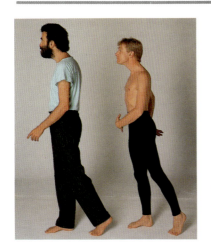

4 Moving to the beat of a different drum.

5 Who's zoomin' who?

6 Jumping for joy.

towards the audience. At the same time you are getting waves of appreciation back from them. A circle of energy is created, giving you a rush of elation.

■ GOOD STANDING

It is strange that we are never taught as part of our basic education how to move with real grace in a way that suits our particular structure. Moving properly during the most simple acts makes it easier to do well at the more complicated ones, such as sports. Moving naturally connects us to nature. Moving consciously gives us a heightened feeling of being alive, as even the simplest of acts take on new depth.

Movement education is easiest to learn when young. By the time we reach our teens we are almost established in our patterns. Still, it is possible to learn new tricks that will assist us in functioning with more economy of movement and that will free energy for other things.

Our bodies have been designed in such a way that when we stand properly we actually do not need to use any muscles to support ourselves, except perhaps the calf muscles. This is quite an incredible point to ponder, because when, as body therapists, we look at people standing they are usually using many of their muscles to maintain their position. Rarely do we come across anyone who stands effortlessly.

Standing easy is a matter of stacking pieces on top of each other. The feet are solidly placed on the ground, giving good support, with the arch in the foot forming a kind of bridge which can carry a huge amount of weight. The ankle, knee and hip joints are built to move easily and to adapt to every shift in the body, keeping balance without tightening up. These joints are meant to be ever flexible and slightly moving, yet most of us grip around the ankle, lock the knees and hold the hip joint tightly. This gives us a false feeling of solidity while actually introducing stress into a body which is designed to be much more fluid.

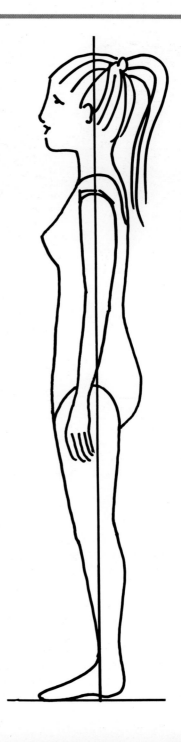

1 Once you've found the ischium bones slowly rock the pelvis forward.

2 ...and backward. Continue rolling like a pendulum but with less and less swing each time.

3 You will naturally come to rest in a relaxed position.

The pelvis is a solid base of support for the whole upper torso. It is built to sit in a certain position, but most people either tip their pelvis forward, producing a sway back, or tuck it under themselves, removing the slight curve that should be there and thereby messing up the whole support system.

The spine snakes out of the pelvis, gently curving its way up the back and supporting the bulk of the body with great ease. When the vertebrae are aligned they can support the bulky weight contained in the torso without having to flex any other muscles of the back or of the belly making them work unnecessarily. Furthermore, when the vertebrae stack up properly, the disks between them are able to do their job, which is to redistribute weight and to absorb and nullify shocks created during movement. When these disks are not in proper balance it is like being in a car with bad shock absorbers; it is a really rough ride that jolts your insides making the muscles tighten up in order to protect the internal organs.

1 Collapsed, unsupported caved into her chair.

2 Much effort is needed producing unnecessary tension.

3 Notice contraction of neck and shoulders.

4 She's up but feeling tight and tired.

The rib-cage grows out of the spine, offering further support for the body as well as protection for the internal organs. The shoulders sit on top of the chest, simply resting there with the arms hanging down, swinging loosely. The shoulders were never meant to hold the body up in the way that many people tend to use them. The whole army stance – shoulders back, stomach in, head held high – is a totally unnecessary and harmful way of standing. Soldiers are killed by their postures, not by their enemies!

The spine ends at the top of the neck. If the head sits truly on top of the neck, as it is supposed to, rather than jutting out forwards or pulled way back, it sits there quite happily on its own without the muscles having to strain at all.

All in all we have an incredibly sophisticated mechanism that is able to support us with no extra effort. Our bodies are a major triumph of engineering that no manmade construction can ever hope to match. Use it wisely and it will serve you well, performing perfectly the many jobs that it was designed to accomplish with the greatest of ease.

■ JUST SIT THERE!

Take a seat in a chair for a minute, sitting away from the back of the chair, so that your spine supports you. In order to find your optimal sitting position first locate your ischium bones. These are rounded bony protrusions in our backsides that provide the base of support when we are sitting.

As you sit on your chair start slowly rocking backwards and forwards, letting your pelvis tilt back and forth. There comes a moment when the ischium bones come into exactly the correct position that will support you.

When sitting, the lower back has more of a natural curve than when standing. This is because the position of the ischium bones give a different

1 Sitting upright and easy with a lower back support.

2 While one foot comes back, the torso swings forward. Back and neck are long, shoulders relaxed.

3 Continuing upward "fall". Notice head in line with body.

4 Up and ready to go.

base of support than your legs would when standing. The lower back has to curve in a bit more to get on top of them.

Once the ischium bones are in the right position it is actually an easy matter to position the rest of the body on top of them by simply stacking up the pieces one on top of the other. You know when you have arrived at the proper position because you are sitting quite straight without making any effort to do so.

■ STAND UP!

Once you are sitting relaxed in your chair, standing up is easy. It is actually more a matter of falling up.

Place one leg more in front and the other closer to your body, perhaps even a bit under the chair. Let the head relax and start to tilt forwards from your pelvis. Keep tilting forwards till it feels like you are about to fall right out of the chair. When your torso is falling forwards directly over your legs, allow the momentum of that movement to enter the legs. Now you effortlessly push up with your calves and suddenly you are standing. Do not use your shoulders and arms to pull you up. They were never designed for that. Do not tense the neck muscles to try and lift yourself up. Falling upwards may seem like a very strange idea at first, and will probably take some practice to get the swing of it, but once you have it, it's the easiest thing in the world.

■ WALKING IN BALANCE

Some people walk leading with their feet, some sway from side to side from the pelvis, some stick the pelvis forwards, while others pull it back. People stick out their chests, jut out their jaws, or even lower their heads and charge through life like a bull. Unfortunately, wrong ways of moving put unnecessary stress on the whole body, opening the door to more serious problems.

We have broken down proper walking into a

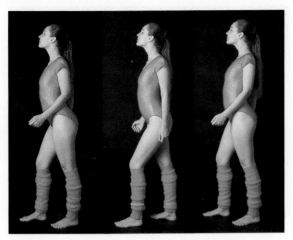

1 Aggressive walk of a fighter. Leading with the chin, while her upper body falls backwards, creating movement in two opposite directions. Note the rigid, clenched fists. What a waste of energy.

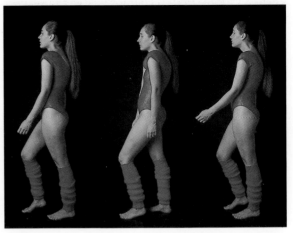

2 The collapsed, depressed walk of the loser. Energy draining out everywhere.

few segments with images to go along with each one:

To loosen and relax the feet and legs, imagine as you walk that it is autumn, the ground is full of fallen leaves, and you are walking through them gently kicking them out of your way. This keeps the ankle, knee and hip joints loose and moving rather than held.

For the proper placement of the pelvis, imagine that you have a long dinosaur tail reaching right down to the ground. The tail is heavy and it keeps pulling your pelvis back under you with each step. But because the tail is wobbling along with you it never pulls the pelvis too far back – just enough to keep supporting the body.

Now imagine that your spine is a string. The string keeps going up until it attaches to your head, which is not a head but a balloon filled with helium. Since helium is lighter than air it keeps wanting to rise upwards. Feel your head being lifted by the helium exerting a slight upwards force from the top of the spine. As it does so it pulls on the spine, not hard enough to make it totally straight and rigid, but just enough to continually bring it up towards a good position. The spine is like a snake, loose and supple and constantly moving yet staying within certain bounds.

All together what we have is a tail pulling you down a bit with a helium balloon pulling you up a bit – the combined effect of which is to bring you to your maximum height without straining – while kicking leaves to keep your legs loose and supple.

Experiment with each image alone till you can feel its effects before moving onto the next one. Then when you have each one happening individually try to bring them all together. Take your time, spreading the whole experiment over several days if you wish. When we are trying to introduce new choices to our bodies it always takes time to override the old conditionings. Be easy with yourself and remember that the whole thing is meant to

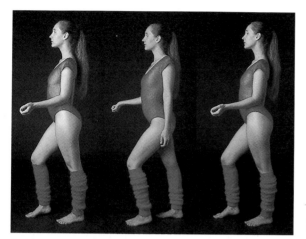

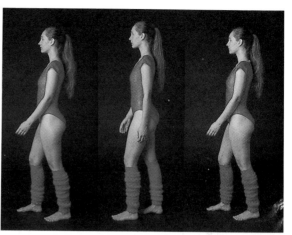

3 Swinging from side to side the seductress looks anything but natural. Her shoulders and hips are rotating unnecessarily.

4 Relaxed and flowing. Every part moving in one direction. Her back is upright without effort as it is supported by her pelvis and legs; her head seems to simply float on her neck. A relaxed and centered walk.

make you more fluid and relaxed, and that trying too hard and getting upset with yourself can only be counterproductive.

■ HEART WALK

Here is one last and very beautiful image to experiment with. Some people walk tough, sticking out their chest and projecting an image of power. Some people collapse and slink along showing an attitude of defeat. Some walk with their heads way forwards, their bodies following behind at a distance, caught in their minds and oblivious to what is happening around them. And there are people who move from their pelvis showing their preoccupation with different sexual ways of being.

The way in which we walk gives a clear indication of our preoccupation at that moment.

The walk we are about to describe is one that comes from the heart and is an indication of our basic humanity and of our love.

Just stand still for a minute and put your hands on the center of your chest in order to feel that place. You will begin to walk with that place as the central point from which you move. Let yourself fall softly forward from the center of your chest. As you begin to fall your legs begin to walk in order to stop you from actually falling down. When you want to walk faster, lean forwards more and when you want to slow down you lean less. If you want to stop you simply do not lean at all and your body comes to an effortless stop.

It is hard to describe, but moving from this place the heart stays open and its energy circulates through the whole body more and more easily. Be sure to breathe fully and deeply during this exercise as the breath allows the heart energy to circulate freely. As this way of walking tends to make people feel more vulnerable you may not want to do it at all times. On a busy street with lots of traffic you may want to adopt a more focused and purposeful stride, but many are the occasions when a heart walk is by far the best way to go.

Locking the knees creates tension, inhibits circulation and puts one off balance. Bending the back puts strain on it. Contracting the neck will surely lead to a stiff neck.

When you bend the knees and ankles the legs will do the work rather than the back, and with a straight back there is less chance of strain.

Remember to bend your knees and use your arms to push the vacuum cleaner (right), rather then moving your pelvis back and forth which will create tension in your back (left).

See if you can spot all the faults and wrong movements of the models (left). Note how much more appealing it looks (right).

ADAPT·ABILITY

As we create more choices in our lives we become more adaptable. The exercises in this book allow us a new flexibility not only in bodily responses but in mental and emotional spheres as well.

As body workers, we have seen this occur many times during the course of sessions, especially in Rebalancing (a system of work on the body which takes emotional, physical, and energetic aspects into account). As an individual becomes more fluid in his body, his whole being undergoes a transformation. There is less struggle and conflict with the changing world, more feeling at ease with whatever comes along.

This does not mean compromising. River water changing direction to move around a rock is not compromising with the thing that stands in its direct path just because it cannot move it out of the way. It simply responds to it and finds a new direction to take.

We are talking about the ability to bend without breaking. There's the story of the eighty-two-year old man, arthritic and barely able to move, who was observed under anesthetic to be so loose in his body that he kept slipping out of the hands of the hospital orderlies who were trying to lift him onto the operating table. These cases are common. Where had the almost immobilized joints disappeared to?

To some extent, they were self-created. Somehow we are programmed to believe that when we are eighty years old and have arthritis we will be unable to move. Fear of damaging an old body might create a self-protective tension which leads to contraction and makes the body more brittle. This in turn would make mobility trickier and may create the very thing the old man fears – a fall. Becoming crippled may be a defense against such a fall, just as it represents an extreme version of a body totally contracted. Under an anesthetic, the built-in programs of contraction, and even of the swelling in the joints that occur in arthritis, were overridden by the let-go effect of the drug.

The limits we meet in our selves, whether our body or our psyches, are self-taught. Psychologically, people are judged insane when they become so confined in the roles they are able to assume that they cannot adapt at all. Senility brings a similar set of limitations. Reality is vast and fluctuating, and constantly inviting or demanding us to meet its variety, but people get stuck in narrow ruts as if they had blinders on. In order to keep up, we need to be as expansive, unfixed and adaptable as possible.

By examining our lives on a regular basis and creating new ways to see and experiment, flexibility (or flowability) comes easily into everything we do.

RELATING TO FOOD

DON'T JUST EAT IT

■ APPETIZERS

Food is fuel for the body – a stimulating experience for the senses. Shared food is a form of relating with our fellow man, eating alone, an opportunity to nourish ourselves. Indisputably, food is a primary need – you are what you eat.

Devoting only five minutes to one or a combination of the following exercises can create the proper atmosphere for eating, and your pleasure and health will both increase accordingly.

The basic premise is simple: to create a small gap between eating and the activities immediately preceding it. Whatever you do before lunch might be boring and sluggish, in which case you will want to tune your body to prepare your metabolism for digestion. If your work has been stressful, exciting or demanding, you will want to unwind before eating.

■ BRISK WALK

A relaxed walk in the fresh air, once around the block, is as effective an exercise as any. It can work both to slow down the pace as it can to pick it up a bit. The only technique is to be as much in the walk itself as possible.

Let the morning's events and the afternoon's plans drop away. Come into the present moment, feel your body from the inside. Pay attention to your stride – let it be loose and relaxed. Feel your whole body stretching and unwinding. Move your arms and hands and head and shoulders.

Like an athlete limbering for the sport, you are warming up, preparing to enjoy the meal ahead.

■ KUNDALINI SHAKE

Take your shoes off and loosen your tie, your belt and anything else you may be wearing that is tight. Be prepared to sweat. Take a couple of deep breaths and begin to gently shake your body.

The emphasis is not on any vigorous effort that tends to shorten and contract the muscles. Rather we are lengthening and loosening the musculature, as well as taking the pressure off the joints of the body. For example, in the arm alone there are joints at the shoulders, elbow, wrist, and three joints in each of the fingers. While shaking the arm all of those joints should be encouraged to move, and to move in as many directions as possible. There is no order to it; the shaking is a random vibration that explores the whole range of nearly effortless movement.

Focus your attention for a while on the arms, until you are satisfied that they are moving easily and fluidly. Then focus on the legs for a while. The thigh muscles, for example, should not be flexed at all but rather in a flapping around mode. Let your head gently shake, keep the jaw slack, eyes almost rolling around in their sockets. See if you can feel the areas of your spine vibrating softly and going in different directions. Shake your pelvis and your behind. Just keep checking the parts of your body and letting them relax more and more. Once you are satisfied that as many parts are mov-

ing in as many ways as possible, then just let it happen by itself without any interference or further focusing. Let your mind be loose as well.

When energy becomes trapped in the body it becomes tension. When tension is left unattended for long periods it becomes chronic and leads to ill health and a bunch of stress-related diseases. What we are doing in this exercise is freeing the trapped tension and letting the energy held in the joints and muscles be released. This technique, done on a regular basis, can go a long way in revitalizing our bodies. Some yogis of old, and many modern-day meditators, use similar methods of shaking and relaxing their bodies to stimulate the cosmic or *kundalini* energy which lies at the base of the spine. When awakened it travels up, eventually to produce an awakening. Certainly when we let our bodies shake in this way – almost like shaking the dust out of a carpet – we feel lighter and clearer afterwards.

After a good five or ten minute shake, some people like to sit still for a few minutes doing nothing. Others prefer to put on some music and dance for a while. Whatever your preference, the kundalini shake is an ideal unwinding and smoothing out the wrinkles exercise before meals, or on arriving home at the end of a day's work.

■ MINI NERVOUS BREAKDOWN

This is at once great fun and a deep emotional cleansing. It is like clearing the circuits of the nervous system. All you need is five or ten minutes in a room without disturbance. A mirror could also be useful. Instrumental music, volume turned up, can help you feel more isolated and disguise some of the noise you may want to make.

Allow yourself to express your nervousness, tension, hurt, or whatever emotions come up for you in that moment. Start by pacing around the room.

Encourage it. Raise your arms and swing your body about. Then follow the following...talk to yourself and make grand gestures. Look in the mirror and make faces at yourself. Growl like an animal. Curl up like a baby. Roll around on the floor. Keep letting go more and more. Stagger like a drunkard. Leap about like a wild creature. Complain, whine and winge. Berate yourself or any imaginary person.

These are all activities you would normally censor in yourself, and probably dislike in others.

1 Stressed out and chaotic "what a mess". Under pressure and ready to crack she's barely keeping it together.

Everyone has some craziness in them, but consciously choosing to let off steam in this way you allow the craziness to surface and end up doing therapy on yourself. Doing it on your own keeps you from dumping whatever hurt, irritability or impatience may come up for you during the day, on other people – your colleagues, friends, and family.

If you're not the type that normally lets off steam in an expressive way, you'll feel a bit self-conscious at first. But give yourself a few minutes and you'll begin to really enjoy carrying on like this, all the more as you're more and more able to totally give yourself permission to hold nothing back.

Issues that seemed serious and overwhelming only moments before will suddenly take on a much lighter air. By the time you emerge from the room to go for your meal, your body and mind are so relaxed that whatever the food it'll taste delicious and agree with your digestive system! If there are issues still left over – say, for example, you got mad at a co-worker in the morning – you might find you simply want to tell them about how you are feeling. Since you will have already shouted at them while

2 Releasing tension in a harmless way...

...breaking out of a rut...

...letting off steam. Very safe and satisfying.

3 Relaxed, released, re-organized.

that – the mind quickly boggles at the very bulk of available information. The fact that the information is often contradictory only adds to the confusion.

The authors have experimented in depth with a wide number of eating habits over the last twenty years, from the extremes of a high protein meat eater's diet with food supplements used by weight lifters and wrestlers, to the non-dairy, sugarless, caffeine-free vegetarian diet of the yoga practitioner. Having inhabited the snowy climate of Canada and the heat of the tropics, having experimented with fasting, colonics, macrobiotics, and a nearly endless range of food fads, we have come to the point of being able to prescribe the perfect diet!

The perfect diet is the one that suits you best! Different people thrive on different foods. What wisdom on the subject we have gathered over the years amounts to that! The responsibility is on the individual to eat in a manner that fits best with their metabolism and disposition, their life style and their taste. By all means experiment: but ultimately, you will become the best authority on what you should eat.

Having said that, here are a few questions to ask yourself. Are meals an enjoyable part of your life? Do you like the taste of the food you eat? Do you feel satisfied when your meal is finished? Are you generally healthy and energetic? Are your bowel movements regular and satisfactory?

If the answer is yes to all these questions then there is no need to tamper with your eating habits, although of course there is always room for improvement. If you have answered no to some of the above you may want to switch around some of your foods. The following tips are only intended as general outlines – food for thought, if you like.

We suggest that whenever you can, take time to eat in a setting that is relaxing and unhurried and aesthetically pleasing. Too much shoveling of food goes on too often in the chaos of fast-food restaurants. Even at home, meal times are frequently

alone in your room, the situation won't be so highly charged and you'll be able to talk to them in a caring way without making an issue of it.

■ EAT AND BE MERRY

The subject of food is close to everyone's heart, not to mention their stomach. Constantly under discussion, if not in the form of Sunday Supplement recipes, then as slimming diets or latest health fads, the gastronomical arts concern us all. New food fashions appear on the scene almost as quickly as women's styles vanish. Unlike clothing, though, they all seem to endure, making eating one of the fastest growing areas of interest .

What is there to eat? Vegetarian, high-fiber, macrobiotic, stress diets, salt-free this, sugarless rushed, accompanied by blaring televisions and other distractions. Take time to do one of the pre-meal exercises, if at all possible, and eat in a caring way. It helps to set out your table in advance with everything you might need, as does taking small bites and eating slowly. One trick to assist you with this is to use chopsticks – it really slows you down! If you are somewhat overweight, everything that you do to bring awareness to your regular eating habits in these ways will help check the problem. Make eating one of your sacred rituals and you'll both enjoy it more and be healthier as a result.

A slow metabolic system would benefit from avoiding meats. Some people thrive on meats and are able to digest them quickly and efficiently. But if it sits in your stomach for a long time, meat will putrefy and cause problems. Fish is probably the easiest of the non-vegetarian foods to digest, with red meats at the tough end of the spectrum.

For a strong digestion, raw fruits and vegetables are very good. A weak digestive system, however, will have trouble with these and want to lean more towards steamed and cooked foods. Lightly steamed is preferable to boiled as steaming preserves the nutrients. It is normal to have a combination of raw and cooked vegetables.

Deep fried foods and fatty or greasy cooked foods are difficult to handle for most stomachs. They are tasty though, and we do tend to want to gobble them up – just check that your gobbling is moderate.

Variety, color, and presentation help in the eating of a satisfactory meal. Even the simplest foods prepared and presented with consideration for proportions different in shape and shade, all create an esthetic harmony that is satisfying to all the senses at the same time. Being happy with what you eat is nourishing in itself; snacks will begin to feel less necessary and some of that compulsive picking at food we all do will drop away. Heavy snackers may like to check to see if something is lacking in their diet that creates the craving for between-meal foods. Watch what you are snacking on and see if you couldn't fit more of those foodstuffs into your meals.

Combining the right foods is an art. Baked beans on toast, for example, is not an English tradition by accident. In a poor household, it was a way of getting a combination that provided a complete protein. In India, dahl (a thick lentil soup) is never eaten without rice and rarely without a chappati, a soft flat whole-wheat bread. In Japan the combination of rice and miso provides the staple protein.

In some parts of the world – in India for example, where the soil is depleted of minerals – one may eat naturally grown food and still find it deficient, and it will need to be supplemented with vitamins and minerals. On the other hand, a balanced western diet should not under normal circumstances require supplementing with vitamins, despite what the trends suggest.

Everyone needs fiber in their diet. It keeps the intestines clean and working efficiently. However you shouldn't normally need added fiber. Some cooked and raw vegetables and fruit eaten each day should be sufficient.

Generally it is easier and healthier to eat a number of small meals through the course of the day than to eat one large meal, especially if that large meal is late at night when the body naturally wants to rest. A large meal, a rich and meaty one, in particular has a long slog ahead down the digestive system, with plenty of work to be done to break it down on the way. Lions eat once every one or two days and loaf about the rest of the time busy digesting. Herbivores, on the other hand, munch small amounts all day long. The proverbial eating like a horse is actually inaccurate – horses do eat all the time, but tiny un-demanding amounts. For human vegetarians, this too would be a more natural way to get their nourishment – if somewhat impractical.

Grains have generally been found to be good for everyone. Rice is a staple in many parts of the world for this reason. Even white rice in conjunc-

tion with other foods seems to provide a balanced and nutritional source, though brown rice is known to be more nutritionally rich.

Local and seasonal foods are the most natural to eat as your regular diet. Imported, frozen, jarred, canned and other such foods are best only in moderation. Of those it is best to eat frozen foods.

It seems to be a good idea to rotate foods. Rather than eating meat for protein at every meal,

for example, try meat a couple of times a week, alternated with fish, tofu, nuts, beans, pulses, eggs and cheeses on the other days.

Some people cannot tolerate dairy products at all. Others can manage only yoghurt which contains enzymes that facilitate digestion. Other people have no tolerance for wheat, still others are allergic to certain foods, nuts, for example.

In the western world, most people eat much more protein than they actually need. It is said that eight almonds provide enough protein to last a day (but don't depend on eight almonds every day). Since protein cannot be stored we need some daily, but there is no use in eating too much as it simply makes extra demands on the digestive system and has to be expelled in the end.

Moderation in alcohol is obviously better than overdoing it; the same applies to sugar, fatty meat, salt, and spices. Stay away from additives and from processed foods as much as possible.

Food-gobbling is a dreadful twentieth-century habit adopted by most people leading busy lives. A significant part of the digestive process happens in the mouth. The more you chew and the slower you eat, the more nutrition you get and the less chance of overeating and upset stomach at the end of the day.

It is actually advisable to stop eating when only two thirds full. It puts less strain on the digestive organs, helps to regulate the weight, and definitely feels more comfortable.

Drink good water. In a hot climate it usually helps to drink a little more than you may naturally have a taste for, especially if you suffer from urinary or kidney problems, or tend to sweat a lot. Avoid very hot and very cold drinks. Some say it is unwise to drink during mealtimes as the digestive juices get diluted as a result and function less efficiently. The exceptions to this though are white wine and naturally fermented champagne, which have an agreeable acidity which aids digestion.

Over-cooking food robs it of its nutritional value. How the British got strong on boiled cabbage is a mystery! Steaming is best, and pressure cooking, performed accurately, also preserves the nutrients in the food.

If at all possible, get into the habit of eating when hungry rather than at fixed times just because everyone else is eating. Hard to do, of course, in western society where eating is such a social habit, but give it a go when you can. It will help you to become more aware of your eating patterns and to know the difference between actually being hungry and eating to avoid being hungry later. But don't let this interfere with your food preparation. You could end up eating nothing but apples!

As you can see, there cannot be any rules about eating. Listen to what your body says rather than your mind – or even the advice of the so-called experts – and as you experiment with different foods and different ways of eating, you will discover what suits you best. And remember that as we grow up our tastes and needs will change. A baby thrives on mother's milk; for a grown man it is not the right food at all. Find your own balance. Try eating one food at a time to see what effect it has on you. You may think you are craving that chocolate bar, but does it really make you feel good, or does the sugar boost you get make you feel worse later? In fact, the craving could be a sign of deficiency in your diet which when modified might make the craving go away.

Finally, remember not to be fanatical. Fanaticism creates a pendulum effect: severe dieting leads to severe gluttony. Hard and strict rules rarely work. Sugar may be bad for you but in moderation almost every system can deal with it. A healthy body can easily manage some extremes, in fact it needs a challenge now and then, it exercises the system and prevents over-sensitivity. Pay attention to your food but not so much attention that it dominates your life. Then you can eat well and have fun with it and stay flexible enough to enjoy eating with others. This is how you stay in balance.

GIVE UP THE FIGHT

Fighting with others, we harm them and in return we are harmed. There can be no real victor. It is the same when we fight ourselves. We become divided, and there can be no winner. It is like the left hand fighting with the right hand, both hands belong to one person, so who will win? Jesus, alone in the desert, refused to take the devil's challenge to compete with him; he let the devil rant and rave and then quietly told him to get lost. By fighting what you see as bad in yourself you merely give it more energy than it has already, and therefore more nourishment to grow. On top of that, the part of you you call good (your right hand) loses its chance of manifesting anything worthwhile by being preoccupied with the part of you you call bad (the left hand). In aikido, a form of Japanese self-defense, the attacker's energy is turned around and used to defeat him. The defender is not aggressive in any way; he simply embraces the energy of his opponent and transforms it.

Embrace is the key word; it is the opposite of fighting. Cease struggling and resisting and try a different stance. Not resignation, collapse or defeat, that is just the negative side of fighting – the reactionary opposite. Learn to embrace life in all its variations and moods, just as you are learning to embrace yourself, and you will have all the forces in life available to you.

MID·AFTERNOON
SLUMP

THE PAUSE THAT REFRESHES

■ RHYTHM WITHOUT THE BLUES

Are you a morning person, up at the crack of dawn, bright eyes and rearing to go? Or perhaps you're a night hawk, one who switches into high gear only after the sun has set. People's energies move in different patterns. Identifying your particular pattern and cooperating with your own body-moods can increase your feeling of being the master of your own life.

By knowing your rhythm, you can avoid making decisions during the slump hours and take things more easily. Peak times are the moments to do your most dynamic activities and most stressful jobs. Of course the routines of the modern world don't always adapt their rhythms to ours, but where you do have a choice, tune in to your body.

These exercises are especially designed for the slump periods everyone runs into during the course of the day. The most common time is the mid-afternoon, but your low times may be different. You know you have hit a slump when everything suddenly goes murky, as if a practical joker had just poured molasses all over you and it's blocking your senses. A couple of cups of coffee and a pastry can give you a caffeine-sugar boost, but this just postpones the slump and actually disturbs your natural rhythm. In borrowing energy from another time of the day and inducing an artificial rush, one eventually ends up more drained and hungover at a time when natural energy would be picking up again.

As often as your life permits it (and find all the nooks and corners of your life that do permit it – more than you'd think at first) allow these periods their natural course without kicking against them. Fighting them tires us out that much more, and you'll find, as you experiment, that there's usually no need for it. Instead, relax into these slow periods as soon as you feel them coming, and let them wash over you. And try a few of these techniques which will assist you in moving through the slump.

■ TWENTY WINKS

If it is possible for you to lie down or even sit in a comfortable chair and drift off for ten minutes, take the time and do it. Just enough to disengage the mind and body, letting it rest without falling deeply asleep.

I knew one guy working a twelve-hour shift who would come up against the depths of his valley at three p.m. like clockwork. Sitting at his desk working with papers he would suddenly find himself dozing, and spend the next two hours struggling to resist actually nodding off on the job. Then one day, alone in the office, he chose to give in to it: he leaned forward on his arms and was gone to the

ZZZzzzzz.......

world. He never slept for more than fifteen minutes and it was usually as little as five. But the mini-siesta was so refreshing that the next time he didn't bother what his coworkers thought and as soon as the eyelids began to droop he stuck a pair of ear plugs in, pulled out a mask from his back pocket, and had his snooze. The result was that immediately after each nap his work picked right up rather than suffering for two hours from the sluggish mind that regularly refused to focus. When he'd established the benefits of this little exercise he went to his boss and checked it out. "Fine by me," said the boss. "Just don't snore, or you'll wake the other people in the office!"

Many people can have this short snooze and be ready to go again. If you lie down, don't get under

the covers – too seductive. Just tell yourself you've got this short time, and you'll most likely wake without a problem. It really works.

■ HANGING

Over the course of the day, as gravity regularly pushes down on us, we find ourselves giving way under the pressure. Our bodies collapse somewhat and the vertebrae in our backs creep closer together. At the end of the day we are actually no-ticeably shorter than in the morning. People have observed that driving home in the evening, they are readjusting their rearview mirrors from its morning position simply because they've shrunk!

We function best when we sit and stand and move at our optimum height. To test this try a simple experiment with two ways of standing.

Start by collapsing your limbs and slumping. Immediately you will feel more tired, perhaps even defeated. Now stand tall – tall remember, not rigid like an army officer – and stay relaxed but at your full height. The straighter you are the easier it is to be energetic and confident. Moreover, it takes less effort to be upright than stooped over.

A simple exercise to regain our full height and to let the back lengthen to its optimum length is to hang for a few moments from a doorway, a bar, or anything high enough to hang from and strong enough to hold you. You need only hang for as long as your fingers can comfortably support you. While hanging let the arms be relaxed. Let the weight of your body do the work, pulling it down. This is a natural traction.

The back muscles must relax for the back to lengthen. Breathe well and with each out-breath let go of the back muscles more and more. This way the stretching happens by itself.

If your feet are not off the ground, place them in front of your body, with heels on the floor. The feet do not have to be up in the air to make the exercise effective, but do not put your feet behind

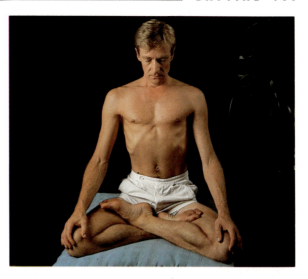

RECHARGING

1 A rejuvenating, energizing, charging up. Do from five to fifteen minutes sitting on the floor or in a chair. Close your eyes and begin. Breathe rapidly through the nose, accent on the inhale, letting your body move with the breath. Continue for five minutes.

2 After five minutes suddenly take a deeper breath - hold it as long as possible and then slowly exhale and relax. If you like, repeat once or twice more.

you, as that will arch your back too much which may aggravate tension already there.

Repeat a few times, giving your fingers a chance to rest. Stand upright and relax while resting.

It is actually a good idea to do this exercise a few times during the course of the day to maintain length in our bodies.

■ ELONGATING

If there is nothing available from which to hang, or at times when you are doing a lot of sitting, perform this simple stretch.

Stand with arms up in the air and alternate your arms reaching for the ceiling. Left arm reaches high, relaxes down. Then the right arm goes up and relaxes down. Meanwhile, to get the maximum stretch, the pelvis on the side that is going up drops downwards. After about ten stretches, five on each side, relax.

Then bend forwards, keeping the legs quite straight without actually locking the knees. Moving down from the waist up, reach for the floor with your hands, but gently. Don't force your fingers to the floor if they won't go there.

Stay in that position, keep breathing and let the movement of the breath along with the force of gravity stretch your back. After a minute, come up again and repeat the upwards stretch.

Another variation you may wish to try is to twist from side to side. Arms out to your side, elbows bent, turn the upper half of your body in one direction while simultaneously turning the lower half of your body the opposite way. If the arms are going to the left, then the left knee bends and leads the lower half towards the right.

Repeat a few times before resuming work; just stand tall and still for a moment, feeling your full height. When you sit, try to retain the feeling of height instead of slumping into your seat. Let the well-being you feel stay with you.

■ BIO-ENERGETICS

Bio-energetics is a system developed by Alexander

❙ Reaching for the ceiling with one hand, while on the same side the knee bends slightly and the pelvis drops.

2 Repeat a few times on each side while inhaling with each stretch.

Lowen for understanding and influencing the whole personality – body and mind together – for resolving emotional problems and increasing our capacity to enjoy life. One of the tools used in bio-energetics is physical exercise that stimulates the movement of energy that is there but not moving. Once the depressed or stuck energy is loosened, the emotional state can also shift more easily.

Below are two of the basic bio-energetics exercises. They are very simple yet their effects can be quite powerful. Through focusing on a held or tense area and actually increasing the tension, we cause the energy to start moving again. This movement is experienced as a vibration or a shaking in the body which you will find invigorating.

Doing both exercises will increase the effectiveness of each. Either start with the first one, or start with the second exercise and repeat it again after you have done the first. This will keep the lower back from getting tight.

■ BACKWARD BOW

Make a fist with both hands and place the fists into your lower back. Stand with feet about eighteen inches (43 cm) apart and the toes turned in. Bend the legs considerably but keep the weight on the balls (the front) of your feet. Arch backwards still keeping the weight forwards on your feet. Breathe through the mouth and into your belly. Hold for a minute letting the vibration in your body go on unhindered.

This exercise releases held energy in the belly.

■ FRONT DROP

Standing with toes pointing in slightly to engage the muscles of the buttocks, and feet about one foot apart (32 cm), bend forward and touch the floor with your fingers without actually putting weight on the hands. Your knees are slightly bent. The weight of the body is in the feet with the head hanging down, loose and relaxed. The breath is

This exercise releases energy in the legs, and these two exercises together will ground you and invigorate you at the same time.

ABOVE Bending forward, keep your legs straight but not locked. Don't strain, let gravity slowly take you down. As the backward bow releases energy trapped in the front of the body, this one stretches and releases energy held in the back.

LEFT Note the smooth curve of the whole body from the ankle up. Hold the position and soon the vibration starts. Keep breathing. If you have lower back pain do this exercise slowly and gently. If the back is aggravated by the position discontinue.

■ CHIN WAG

We have included this technique in the mid-afternoon slump section though it can be done a few times during the course of your day. It is ideal for nearly any situation because it takes only a few moments to complete.

Nearly all of us have tight jaw muscles. They are very short, extremely strong muscles that get a lot of use, and tend to accumulate and store a great deal of tension. When we repress an emotion, when we grin and bear it no matter what it is, we use the jaw muscles to do it. A stiff upper lip is accomplished with the help of the jaw muscles. Any time we want to say something and stop ourselves, and whenever we try to keep some outside energy from entering, the jaw muscles are involved – we become tight-lipped. Then once a cycle of tension is established, even such common activities as eating, talking and even laughter can add more tension to the area. In some cases people grit and grind their teeth at night, which is an unconscious effort to get rid of the tension. Sometimes the entire mouth and teeth are deformed by these muscles. But tension in the jaw is so common that most people are suffering from it without even knowing it.

Locate these muscles by placing your fingers on the sides of your face and opening and closing your mouth a few times. You may not realize that these are muscles at all because they feel so rock hard. Now press your fingers or knuckles into them. Once they are pressed some way, move your fingers a bit, still maintaining the pressure. Try strumming across the muscles (they run up and down, so you are strumming sideways, that is towards your nose and away from it). If you are doing it correctly you will notice several things happening. First of all, it hurts. This is a sign of the

easy, moving through the mouth, and it is a little deeper than usual.

Slowly put the weight on the balls of your feet, the heels may rise into the air a bit. At the same time you are straightening the hamstring muscles in the back of your legs. Do this without locking or totally straightening your knees. Hold for a minute and then relax.

During this time some trembling or vibration should have begun in your legs and possibly in your whole body. If not, don't worry. A few days of experimenting will get you into the swing of it.

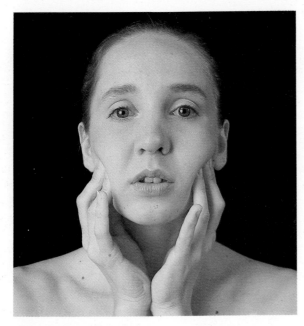

There really is muscle there.

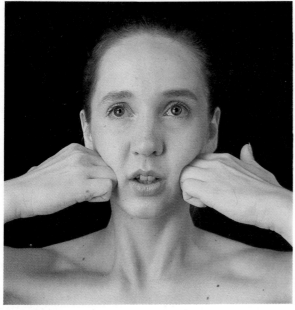

If your fingers are weak, try your knuckles.

tension there. Second, it either makes you hold your breath, or you begin to breathe deeper. Some people take a sudden gasp of air. Encourage the breathing and not the holding of the breath.

Holding on is what we are already doing; as we tense, our breathing becomes more and more controlled and shallow. The shallow breathing means less oxygen and carbon dioxide interchange within the body, which in turn makes us tired and sluggish. Massaging your jaws is like a breath of crisp, fresh air. It wakes us up. Like any sudden shock it puts the body on alert, clears the mind and prepares you for action. At the same time, because you are releasing energy instead of accumulating it, you feel more relaxed afterwards. What more can you ask from a thirty-second workout?

If, as recommended, you do this exercise a few times during the course of your day, especially during tense and trying times, your jaw will start off by becoming more sensitive and achy. This won't last for more than a week. The massage will relax the muscles and the ache will go, and you'll stop feeling pain in the jaw while doing it. You'll still get a strong sensation as you do it and it will continue to affect the breathing and the rest of the body, but it won't hurt anymore.

If it does not hurt when you first begin to work on the jaw muscles, it probably means that you are not doing it hard enough. The object of the exercise isn't to cause pain, of course, but the amount of pain indicates whether you are penetrating deeply enough to allow the muscles to loosen. Proceed slowly at first. Cooperate with your breathing, and go deeper and deeper. Some people cannot seem to be able to go deeply enough into their jaws at the beginning. If that is the case for you, ask someone else to do it for you. Get them to stop when the pain gets too much. But it is better to do it to yourself, or to get an experienced body worker to assist you. Trust your own senses; no damage can be done if you listen to your body. After a few times you will actually enjoy the release of tension and its invigorating effects.

RESPONSE-ABILITY

Living in balance means owning your difficulties and taking responsibility for yourself. This might seem like an obvious statement, yet, increasingly over the last decades mankind has been abdicating responsibility to specialists in every field. Politician, advertiser, designer, psychoanalyst – everyone has a system to pontificate about: a set of clothes all should look good in, or a series of theories into which the personal rumblings of our unconscious must fit to match.

Even book-knowledge is just about useless when it tries to take the place of direct experience – which is why this book constantly invites you to experiment for yourself. Otherwise, filled with noise from magazines, radio and TV, who will hear the birds singing in the early morning?

Of course the specialists will argue that the world has become so complex and so packed with rapidly changing information, that no one can know what is really going on without their help.

For example, look at the way we have put all our faith in the power of science. Science appears to know so much more than us that we've thrown away our trust in our own common sense in favor of its theories. Whereas, in fact, science is simply a tool for a particular kind of understanding of our universe. By dissecting every fact and breaking it into its smallest possible components, the scientists make us believe that they can help us understand the essence of anything. But although science may have no problem splitting the atom or producing a more sophisticated coffee-maker, when it comes to our personal fulfillment, it's up to us.

Having said that, we refer to the advice of yet another type of expert, the mystic. All the religions may argue, disagree and fight it out on the streets of Belfast or Bierut, but if we examine the message of almost any mystic, regardless of religious affiliation, we perceive a common thread. In all their varied forms of expression, the mystics do appear to agree that life is a voyage of discovery, a mystery to be lived through, rather than a problem to be solved.

They teach by example: know thyself, seek and you shall find, the kingdom of God is within. They throw the onus of responsibility back on the individual. They seek to empower us rather than strip us of our natural God-given energies.

Just what does it mean to take responsibility? Simply put, it is acknowledging that at any given moment, in fact in every moment of our lives, what we choose is of our own creation. We and only we are in charge of ourselves.

Of course there are plenty of arguments against this: heredity, environment, reasons of race, color and creed, IQ, karma... there are lots of excuses why we cannot take responsibility for our actions.

Outside influences do affect us, it is true. But it is equally true that it is we who control how we respond to these influences. We have all known days when everything goes our way, as well as days when nothing goes right. Is it just coincidence, or is it actually something we are putting out, some energy or vibration we are emanating? Each of our responses to events in the world around us is uniquely individual. It is our response – we own it. And the quality of our responses affects life around us.

It may be hard to realize that the quality of our response depends largely on our conditioning.

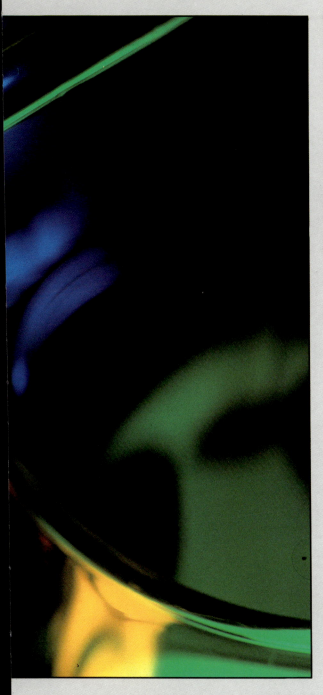

What one person may find offensive may be a delight to someone else. There is no definitive definition of what is unpleasant, although many of us will agree on many things: war for instance, at least officially, is considered bad. But there are plenty of folk in cultures other than ours who lap it up; it alerts the adrenalin for one thing. An aristocratic English lady, for example, may be offended if a man fails to offer her his seat when she enters the room, but a radical New Yorker may be offended if he does.

In the same ways as we are divided within our cultures, we are divided within ourselves.

Experiment at times when you are dogged by indecision or by contradictory feelings by owning who you are at every junction where your mind swings into reverse, and by taking responsibility for the direction you're going at that moment. The enthusiastic and well-intentioned jogger that sets the alarm for 5:30 a.m. is not the same person as the groggy sleeper who reaches out and turns it off without even waking up. Yet both exist with equal force. By taking responsibility for the different characters we find inside ourselves we can strike an agreement that is mutually satisfactory.

Perhaps we jog during lunch, for example. If we don't do this, one personality will be frustrated and get his own back. Maybe the sleepy guy gets overruled by the jogger only to take revenge by tripping him up and spraining his ankle. Well of course it wasn't Jogger's fault – he didn't see the sidewalk suddenly ending. Probably because at that moment Groggy was too busy complaining about having to imitate Jogger to notice. Now Jogger could be even more furious and berate Groggy for giving him a sprained ankle and making sure he can't run at all, by calling himself stupid and making himself miserable as a result. Once again owning that there's a Fool inside him, and a cheerless little fellow called Misery ready to winge at the slightest thing, and owning these bits of himself and taking responsibility for their existence, is all that needs to happen.

It is because we are judgmental about these other characters that don't fit with our image of ourselves that we don't like them, and it's because we don't like them that we ignore them. But being left out is one thing they won't stand for. For example, an extremely bullying Jogger might continue to run despite the sprained ankle, once again refusing to acknowledge and take responsibility for the sleepy guy inside him who really doesn't want to run at all, and this way end up doing even more serious damage to his body.

At every juncture, owning who we are would mean recognizing the message in the sprained ankle and giving permission for that sleepy fellow to sit with his leg up for a bit. Try having a moment-to-moment dialogue with yourself, and create an understanding that takes into account all the players within you that often have conflicting ideas. Now if the jogger is totally fed up with owning himself, and wants a stiff drink to drown out the internal dialogues, fine, give him a stiff drink, and take responsibility for that too! You are a free human being. Taking full responsibility for the consequences of your actions will be as vital as taking responsibility for the actions themselves.

PART III
EVENING

AFTER WORK

PLAY

■ JOGGING

Books have been written on it, shoes built for it, clubs opened around it, and even food supplements have been concocted solely for those who do it. The craze, already a decade old, is as fashionable as ever – from teen-agers to retired couples everyone jogs. Yet, as we see it, very few people actually get the best from this great form of body movement.

What follows is by no means a complete guide to jogging. Rather, it consists of a few general observations gathered from many years' work with joggers and is designed specifically for the experienced – whether seasoned marathon runners or weight-watchers who are just running round the block.

Before starting any sporting activity, a good warm-up involving loosening and stretching the muscles is vital. This is so if you're going to prevent muscle ache and decrease the chance of damaging yourself with sudden activity unfamiliar to the body.

While you're at your stretches take the opportunity to clear your mind a bit, shedding the thoughts of the day. The day claims all your attention except while you're jogging; let this time be your private vacation.

Choose your setting.

One friend loved to run through Manhattan. When he was over the shock of carbon fumes, there was a thrill in remaining attuned to his own running pace and still alert to the threat of the hundreds of street activities going on around him. Running without either coming to a standstill or falling under a car was the main challenge of his day!

Most of us, however, just enjoy an invigorating jog along the sidewalks of suburbia – pick your setting carefully. If you can, run in a park, on a beach or through the countryside. Relaxing environments invite you to atune yourself to nature – not just to the vibrant animal in your body, but to the gentle living world around you. Out in the fresh, you'll be comfortable with your deep breaths and in harmony with the scenery.

Start by having a good time. As is clear from the faces of those seen straining at the calves, at least half the joggers on the road have forgotten this vital ground rule. If you've been jogging for a month or so and it is still a chore you can't wait to complete, then maybe it is not for you. Find another physical activity you genuinely enjoy.

Don't be goal-oriented. Sometimes we are motivated into doing strange things with our bodies (such as aimlessly running with it) because we need to lose some pounds or are worried about our backaches and want to get fit. These are good enough reasons to get you out on the road at the beginning; certainly jogging can be great for both the body and the spirit. But if you persist in running just to get in shape or to prove something to your neighbor, you will probably strain yourself and end up doing more harm than good.

Start out easily, don't plan a long route, stay relaxed, and find pleasure in the activity of your limbs and muscles. The more you can simply be present to the moment without thinking about where you're going or how long it's going to take you, the more the sheer beauty of jogging will be revealed to you.

Take it easy. There is no need to overexert yourself. Remember that each person's individual limits are vastly different and to compare your body's activities with another's is meaningless. As you run, your endurance and your speed increases naturally. Feel your own pace; trust in the feel of your own pace. One day down the line you may wish to compete or run marathons, but running is a gentle process and marathons are not for everyone.

One of the most effortless ways to run is by first allowing yourself to fall forwards from the ankles – slowly at first – and then catching yourself. As you go faster you fall more and catch yourself quicker. In this way you will find yourself expanding as you run rather than contracting. You open rather than close.

Avoid jarring. Jogging can be a smooth wave-like motion or a thumping motion that shakes up your guts and hurts your joints. Feel yourself as you run; meet the ground softly and let the wave gather through your body. Try becoming a ballerina for five minutes. If you study other joggers you will immediately see a difference between a fluid runner and one who jars and causes friction in his body.

Release through the hips. Try to feel from the inside what it is like to barely lift your leg. Instead release it outwards, lengthening it away from the torso. If you do the falling and catching technique there won't be any jarring and you will notice the legs lengthening outwards of their own accord, rather than tensing.

Feel the places where you hold. Pay attention to your arms; let them relax and swing loosely. Shake out your fingers, wiggle your shoulders for a moment, and feel them move. Running downhill with completely loose shoulders and arms flapping makes a great self-massage for that usually tense part of the body – the shoulders.

Allow the pelvis to swing. Climb into it for a minute or so and feel it swinging from the inside! Loosen your head; drop the jaw and let it be relaxed. Just pay attention to each area and if it feels tight, let go of it. Imagine it as a part of the body that can fall away, that can actually detach itself and drop off from your fulcrum. Move from one area to another in this way.

By consciously putting your attention into different parts of your body at moments when you are engaged in highly charged activities, you will find it comes more naturally to do so at other times, when you are less inclined to remember your body.

Feel the breath and play with it. Try a double breath: two breaths in through the nose and two out through the mouth. Experiment with different rhythms. Your lungs are being exercised whether they like it or not. Might as well like it.

Running is not just one hurried plod after another. It's your body discovering itself. So change the rhythms and see what happens. Sprint for a while, then slow down again. Make some effort and then forget effort altogether. Go with the fluctuations of your moods. Walk for a bit, then run some more. Try stopping dead altogether – totally: fix your limbs, close your eyes, relax, and do nothing but listen.

Change the focus of your attention. One moment you're aware of nothing but the multiple feelings in your body, the next your attention is on the blossoms on the trees or the setting sun. There's no need to get fixed on any one thing. There is no right way except to do what feels good and to be open to changes.

When jogging is enjoyable we fall into a kind of harmony with ourselves and our surroundings – what is known as the runner's high. You may lose weight, tone up your muscles and transform your-

Movement is freedom.

self into an irresistible member of the opposite sex, but without the expansive sense of well-being that comes about through jogging, you may as well sit at home.

■ PRIME TIME TV TIPS

"The Medium is the Message" – *Marshall McLuhan*

Television can be a curse or a blessing – the choice is ours. Without a doubt, it is radically affecting the structure of our lives. It takes us to deepest Africa without mosquitoes or to the Antarctic without the cold. Along with the jet plane, it makes the world a global village.

Its simple entertainment is seldom challenging or disturbing, rarely brilliant (except perhaps in the U.K.), and yet it can relax us. In fact on one level it over-relaxes – it turns the viewer into a vegetable.

Television in no way urges our creativity to emerge, it assaults our eyes and ears while all other senses are ignored. And at the same time as it brings us closer to the outside world, it alienates families. They may be sitting together in the same room and yet alone and involved with the TV set instead of with each other.

This, however, is a situation that can be remedied. The following suggestions attempt to do just that.

If you have a video machine, what could be better than making full use of it to record your favorite TV shows rather than making yourself a passive consumer of whatever comes up on the screen? Take time off to check out your *TV Guide* and systematically set the video to cover those programs you know you don't want to miss. Now you're in charge.

Try turning the video off in the middle and taking a deliberate break. Go for a walk, chat with someone in the house, come back into yourself, and then resume the program. With video you have more control over what happens: if you miss a sequence you can rewind and see it again, if you're bored you can fast forward. Sit comfortably.

Bad slouchy posture while watching TV means that any pain in your body will be intensified. It is worth having a good chair with adequate back support. Change positions often so that you do not get fixed in any one place. Take a few deep breaths and come back into your body. When you deliberately blink a few times while watching TV you become less caught up with what you are seeing. This is especially good for those horror movies that threaten to keep you awake at night!

Touching is one of the most intimate ways of relating. While watching television we have the perfect opportunity to practice this art. Sitting side-by-side with another person, husband, wife, chil-

Use your time in front of the TV constructively. Don't become a vegetable.

dren, or friends, take up his or her hand and massage it. Or, opposite each other on the couch take turns massaging each other's feet. After a hard day standing on one's feet for hours, getting a foot massage is near to paradise!

One person sits on the couch and the other on the floor in front, and the position is ideal for massaging stiff shoulders, neck, scalp and jaws. Scalps love to be touched, but seldom are. Try to actually move the scalp around a bit, pinching, rolling, slight friction, even gently pulling the hair, all feel incredible. It relaxes the head and everything in it, improves circulation and helps prevent hair falling out.

Talk to the people watching with you. Relate in

other ways too, during the show, especially if it's the kind with its own interludes, like the news or the football game. During sports it's great fun to do your own commentary, to cheer your team on, and to curse the bad plays. Don't let yourself get too passive!

It's worth shutting the set off from time to time even if you're going to turn it on again a few minutes later. You feel back in control again.

In front of the TV, do a few of those little things that don't take much physical energy or deep concentration: floss your teeth, knit, polish your shoes, do that mending that's been waiting in your closet for days, brush your hair, or brush someone else's hair. The possibilities are endless.

KID IN A CANDY STORE

As you experiment with the techniques presented in this book you will be discovering new choices coming into your life. You will be living with increasing variety, and variety really is what gives spice. Variety opens new doors of experience and growth, and at the same time, it closes the doors on boredom and routine.

Of course, some routine is beneficial in our life. There is already enough chaos and insecurity in the world today, and most people prefer to live a life of order. But there does, as in all things, need to be a balance. Too much order and familiarity makes us sleepy and less alive than we would like to be.

The perfect balance is one that has the elements of routine as a base with plenty of variety thrown in to add the unpredictability we need to stimulate us. We tend eventually to react to too much order by swinging the other way, and this swing, if it happens too unexpectedly, can be harmful. An article in a British newspaper illustrates this point. A highly placed civil servant of thirty years standing strangled his wife. They had a dispute over where the mustard container should be placed on the kitchen table. For years it had stood on the same spot. Suddenly one day the wife wanted to place it on the other side of the table. The man was so enraged at this change in routine that, before he had realized what he was doing, he had killed the woman he had been married to for thirty-seven years. Upon being questioned by police, the man said, "It was her fault. She insisted on moving the mustard. I don't know

what happened. I saw red and the next thing I knew she was dead."

The example is somewhat extreme but serves well to illustrate the point. We can fall so deeply into routine that we cannot stand to see it disturbed. And so unaware was this man that he had no idea what he was doing. His reaction was that of a somnambulist, a sleepwalker.

The spirit of our exercises is one of exploration and of fostering a curiosity in the workings of our bodies, minds and feelings. Allow this curiosity to spread into the day-by-day structure of your life. Variety does not have to be of a dramatic nature. Existence loves variety. Why else would it bother to make every snowflake unique and different? Life is an abundance of variety, much of it extravagant and without any real functional purpose. It is there simply because it is beautiful to behold in all its differences. If we can remain open and available to the incredible variety all around and within ourselves, our lives will be immensely enriched.

■ UP IN SMOKE

This is an exercise for those who smoke. However, if you are a nonsmoker, it is possible to adapt it to any kind of habitual behavior in order to gain a deeper understanding of it.

Let's look at my reality and possibly yours. I smoke. We all know that smoking is hazardous to health. What many of us smokers don't consider is that aesthetically speaking, it is an ugly habit: in many ways more offensive than flatulence since it endures a lot longer and is considerably less healthy for all. It makes my breath and clothes stink, and when I light up I fill the room, and the faces and lungs of everyone in the room, with this offensive smell – no matter what the Marlboro man says. For these reasons, part of me would like to stop.

Another part does not. This part is also divided into several subsections. The habit itself compels me to light up. Furthermore, I feel a strong resistance to being told what I should and should not

do. I cringe, especially in the presence of those who have recently stopped themselves and are now on a holy crusade to convince others to do likewise. Call it sheer stubbornness or childishness, I won't deny it, right now that's the way I feel. Finally, there is part of me that enjoys smoking. A good smoke at the end of a meal with a fine brandy... the simple pleasures of life.

All in all, my smoking self seems to be schizophrenic. Smoke... no, don't smoke... let's stop... I can't... you can... I won't. And on it goes *ad nauseam*. This type of behavior gives rise to a certain loss of self-respect. One feels like a slave to habit rather than being master of oneself.

The following exercise does not condemn smoking. Rather it is aimed at a deeper understanding of ourselves, and for that reason we do not judge the habit. Instead we try to smoke more consciously, more totally, with the aim of getting to know what it means to us. During the exercise there are no internal warring factions, so we give ourselves permission to be total, whole and integrated. And wholeness strengthens and fulfills. Perhaps it is this very fulfillment we seek when we light up. Experiment and see what happens for you.

To begin with, you will have to do this exercise alone. Sit in a comfortable place where you will not be interrupted with a pack of your favorite cigarettes, pipe or cigar, and a lighter. Examine the pack for a few moments, feel its reassuring fullness, and enjoy the packaging and the look of it. Then slowly choose and remove a cigarette. Do it slowly. Tap it on a hard surface to pack the tobacco for a more even smoke. Smell the tobacco to ascertain whether it is to your liking. I have a package of John Players Special before me: rather elegant packaging and the aroma of the cigarette brings back some vague and mixed memories.

Now, light a match or lighter of your choice. Take a moment to examine the flame before bringing it to the cigarette and lighting up. Inhale deeply, letting the warm smoke be sucked down

your throat and into your lungs. Exhale slowly, and watch the smoke curl through the air, visible one moment and gone the next. Be in all your senses. It is an essential part of this exercise to give all your attention to it. Do not do anything else but smoke and experience the smoke. Be thinking of nothing else! Smoke as much of the cigarette as you feel like and when you stub it out stub it out deliberately. If you want another one, go right ahead and have it. Just be sure to do it slowly and consciously. And give yourself permission to enjoy the whole act totally. Just for now, have no thought, and suspend all judgment. Just be with it and see how it feels to you right now.

That is all there is to it. No great insights or revelations are necessary. A simple act done just for itself.

As I did it just then I did enjoy it, for the first few puffs at least, and then the smoke began to irritate the back of my throat and I put it out. A few minutes later, having forgotten about the irri-

By paying attention to every detail you give yourself a choice.

tation and remembering the pleasure, I reached slowly for another one. This time, just as I was about to light up, I became aware of a slight shortness of breath left over from the first one. So I stopped, put down the cigarette and just began to breathe deeply for a while, relaxing my throat and lungs while stocking up on a bit of oxygen. This actually led me to standing up and moving about and stretching my body. As I did this, I became aware that at this moment my body did not feel ready for another smoke. Then I asked my mind if it wanted to smoke just then. There was no pressure, no shoulds and buts present. My mind felt quite relaxed and in harmony with my body. The idea to smoke had receded into the background. I went for a stroll instead.

During my stroll something dawned on me that I had heard before, except now it had a real impact on me because I was personally experiencing the truth of it. Often when we smoke it is actually something else that we want to be doing. The smoke is a substitute. The body is hungry and eating is inconvenient, so we smoke instead. We can be tired and smoke to wake up, and strangely enough, we smoke to make ourselves sleepy as well. We feel lonely and smoke for companionship, or we feel nervous and smoke to hide it or to repress it or even to show others that we are nervous so they will have mercy on us. We can smoke to show that we are cool or that we are hot. In the ads, smokers are shown to be in turn rugged, sensitive, gay, pensive, social and loners. It expresses a vast range of feeling and mood.

The real problem arises, however, when the habit becomes so deeply ingrained and so unconscious that we substitute a smoke for some other act, before even realizing what we wish to be doing!

If I am hungry, nervous, tired, afraid, excited, or bored, and choose to smoke, that's okay. But if I am not really aware of the force behind the act and just light up, I am missing something in my life. I am becoming a robot. This was the basic

To smoke or not to smoke.

realization on my little walk. Just feeling the truth of it in that moment gave me fresh resolve to pay more attention to my habits. And it gave me a strength which in turn gave my feet extra bounce and life.

The real significance of this exercise you, like me, will have to discover for yourself. That's the fun and challenge of it. It does not work to read and believe what someone else says. Even the medical warning on the packet of cigarettes I cannot heed. It only triggers the rebellious part of me. I have to feel within my body the adverse effects and make my own choices. The child has to touch fire before it really gets the message that fire causes pain. Does this mean that I will have to get bronchitis before I stop smoking? I hope it does not get to that. Let's see what happens next!

For a bit of inspiration, I share with you some of the things the exercise has done for me. I smoke less, because each one is more satisfying. When I smoke this way I relax in myself more and actually feel better about the ones I do smoke. I feel less schitzy. I often put out cigarettes after a few puffs because at that moment it does not satisfy me to smoke. Often, as happened in the previous story, I realize what it is I really want to be doing, or what I am avoiding doing. Sometimes then I do it. And even if I do not, at least I have the choice! I feel less mechanical, less a slave, more real. I have not stopped smoking; instead I feel myself moving towards a state of inner balance and inner health which is by its very presence changing a lot of my habits.

We believe that if you do even just this exercise in a wholehearted way it can change your life and start you on a fresh course. Do not get discouraged if it does not happen for you right away. Keep giving yourself the time and space to experiment. And even though it has had a big build-up of sorts, try not to have any expectations about it. This advice may seem paradoxical at first. It is not. Expectation is one of the main forces that removes us from experiencing the moment. When is it going to happen? Am I doing it right? It's never going to work for me. I am too stupid to get it. I am too smart to fall for it.

Everyone has these thoughts. I know I did, and still do even though I know it works. The trick is to suspend judgment and especially to suspend judgment of judgments themselves. They arise, you notice them and pay no attention. Do not feed the habit; enjoy the smoke. Enjoy the moment. And do not struggle if you try and nothing happens. So what?

Don't get into the habit of giving yourself a hard time. A little perseverance, another try, yes, another smoke consciously and you are bound to get it. It just happens: suddenly you are there, just smoking, or, just not smoking. It's a great feeling.

What is meditation, and what has it got to do with smoking?

True meditation is doing absolutely nothing. It

1 Simply hold the head without covering the ears.

2 Explore the whole area around the eyes.

is putting the mind to rest, stopping all thought processes, and just being in the moment. (See *Meditation: Simply Sitting*)

Smoking in many ways is pretending to do something while actually doing nothing. All one is doing is a type of breath exercise. Taking breath into your body and sending it back out again.

Meditation techniques include breathing exercises, chanting mantras, visualizations, prayers, and yoga positions. None of them is really meditation, for meditation involves no doing at all. However, these techniques can be helpful in bringing one into the realm of meditation. And in this way smoking can be used as a meditation technique.

And the fun thing about smoking is that one can do it anywhere at any time. At parties, in restaurants, anywhere where smoking is possible. Once we have practiced by ourselves, we can do smoking meditation technique any time we choose.

Smoke and really feel your body. Smoke to be quiet and just be with yourself in the middle of a crowd. If you suddenly start chanting, people will give strange looks and bother you. But who pays any attention to someone just sitting and having a quiet smoke. Remember the cigarette I mentioned earlier, the one with brandy after a good meal? It can be a very relaxing, almost mystical, smoke. As if for those moments all is right with the universe.

This is what the advertisements promise but fail to deliver. We, on the other hand, can make it happen for ourselves.

It has been said that smoking satisfies a deep-seated desire for the mother's breast and its warm, nourishing milk. A desire that was not completely fulfilled when we were infants. Sucking on the cigarette reminds us of the breast, and the movement of the warm smoke, of the mother's milk. However, the cigarette is a poor and unhealthy substitute. A big round, glowing pipe may be a better one. However, in the privacy of your own home lay even better substitutes. The obvious one, of course, is the real thing. Here is another, and for some who have experimented with it, it has led to satisfying the craving and an end to smoking.

Simply get a baby bottle, make the hole in the end a bit bigger, fill it with the warm liquid of your choice, and enjoy! Just in itself it is a very relaxing and satisfying activity and will allow you to contact very early childhood spaces when life was much more simple and basic.

■ FACE MASSAGE

The face – doorway to our personalities and mirror of our souls. It is the most exposed area of our bodies. More of our sensory apparatus is stored there than anywhere else. Constantly in use, the main means by which we are recognized and identified by others, the face is a vessel for much beauty and strength. But because of its intricate composition, it is also an area that stores a great deal of tension. Furrowed brows, straining eyes, clenched jaws, stiff upper lip: these are only a few of the obvious manifestations.

Following is a massage that can be done in ten minutes or luxuriously drawn out for much longer. What makes it more exciting is that you can practice it either on yourself or on another person. By doing it both ways you can experience which strokes feel the best and are the most effective.

Take the basic format of this face massage and with practice adapt it to suit your own style.

The exercise describes one person massaging another. You can also do it on yourself however you wish – in the office, in the bathroom, anywhere. See how quickly your face responds by feeling more vibrant. Soon you will come to sense how the whole body is affected by it.

The person you are working on should lie on a comfortable supporting surface. Make sure they are warm and secure. Place their head on a pillow or, even better, in your lap.

For a few moments simply hold the head without covering the ears. Don't do anything; just feel

3 Stroke outwards over the cheek bones.

4 Sometimes it is enough just to hold your partner's face for a few moments.

the nurturing part of yourself and give the other a chance to tune in to your touch. Focus on the moment.

Take a soothing oil or lotion and make sure it's not too cold on your partner's skin. You can bring it to body temperature by rubbing it into the palms of your hands. You will be using this oil to soften your massage gestures, and bearing in mind that the face has the highest concentration of nerve endings in the body, be aware of the state of your own hands and remember not to stretch or drag the other's skin too much.

Place your thumbs or the flat of the hand on your partner's brow and gently stroke along the hairline. You will quite likely notice an immediate response: the breathing becomes deeper and more serene; maybe there is the release of a sigh or two; there might even be a change in coloration as the blood flows more easily.

With your fingers, gently but firmly press on the bony rims of the eyes. There is no movement necessary, just press and slowly release. Explore the whole region around the eyes, pressing and releasing, and remembering to stay only on the bone and to steer clear of the eye itself.

Rub your palms together vigorously until they are quite warm and cover the eyes so that the palms make contact with the eyelids. Don't press on the eyes; just rest your hands there.

Feel the place where the nose meets the forehead and cheeks, massaging and wiggling the area, using some force but still moving gently.

Starting from the nose, stroke outwards over the cheek bones, over the temples and into the hair.

Find the jaw muscles and massage them with the tips of your fingers. Sometimes deeper pressure applied to these jaw muscles releases a lot of tension. Experiment going deep into your own jaw muscles to see how it feels. (For more on jaws, see *Chin Wag*.)

Stroke the lips from the center outwards, top and bottom. Follow the jaw-line right up to the ears. Carefully and lightly stroke the throat. When you get to the sides and back of the neck where it is more muscular and less sensitive, you may go deeper to relieve some of the tensions that are invariably held there.

Keep experimenting on yourself to find out how deep you can safely go in different regions of the head and neck. If your touch is too light, it may be ineffectual.

Finish off by massaging the scalp. The scalp is an often-neglected area that actually loves to be worked on. It's well known that hairdressers who throw in a bit of massage with their soaping have no shortage of clients! Try to actually lift the skin off the skull and move the scalp around in both small circular movements and light pinching movements.

When you are done, allow your partner an undisturbed few minutes to enjoy their new face. You too might like to stay as you are and rest with them.

Take care not to be in a hurry as you do your massage. It is preferable to go for fewer strokes instead of rushing hurriedly through them all. You can even take moments to rest by placing your hands on the top of your partner's head or shoulders. With practice, this massage becomes almost a single smooth-flowing gesture, with one step giving way naturally to the next. Notice how it is as nourishing for the masseur as it is for your partner.

■ OCTOPUS

A very happy participant christened this exercise the octopus and if you try it, you will soon understand why. Three, four or even more people take turns giving and receiving a massage. One person receives, while the hands of all the others massage and nurture all together. The combined efforts of four, six or even eight hands provide the octopus effect.

Four is probably an ideal number as it gives everyone a chance to receive without having to

wait very long. We found that with four people twenty minutes each is a good time. With three people thirty minutes is fine. Four times twenty minutes, plus some time for relaxing and changing over, clocks in a little under two hours: a very pleasant evening's entertainment. With more than four people the time starts to get a little long, as twenty minutes is a minimal time to enjoy receiving a massage of this kind. Still, with over four people some can be taking a little break or making tea for variety and rest.

A massage table or any suitable raised surface is ideal. The massage can be done on the floor, but a table is more convenient and saves having to bend over as well as making moving around easier. Prepare the space beforehand by putting on some nice music and dimming the lights or using candles and perhaps some pleasant light incense. Have a nice oil or some lotion on hand.

One of the beauties of this massage is that no-one really has to be proficient in massage technique. The quantity of hands working makes up for lack of expertise. The key is to remain sensitive to the person on the table and to your massage partners.

Begin slowly, placing warmed-up hands on the person. If your hands are cold, put a little oil on them and rub together to warm them up. Also make sure the room is warm and snug. The art is in moving together, slow and easy, and finding a rhythm with your partners that turns the whole process into a dance. Indeed, as you massage, allow your whole body to move and sway and be soft. The softness and fluidity translates through your hands into the body of the person on the table. Use any style that you are comfortable with. Some people like to move around, covering large areas, while others concentrate on smaller surfaces in depth, perhaps a foot, a hand or the face. Stay sensitive to the tissue under your hands and it will tell you how to proceed, sometimes asking for deeper work, other times telling you to go lighter or slower. Don't be afraid to jiggle the body, to pick

up an arm or a leg and gently shake or rotate it, or even just to rest your hands for a while on one part of the body and just breathe. Even a relaxed touch is soothing and healing. About halfway through the massage – and it is good to time it – ask the person whether they would like to turn over. Most people do like to have both back and front touched but a few are so comfortable they prefer not to move.

A satisfying way to finish is for one person to hold the head, another the feet, while a third covers the body with a sheet. This signals to the person on the table that time is nearly up without disturbing them by talking. After the sheet is in place, just leave him lying on the table undisturbed for a few minutes before changing over. It feels very good for the person on the table to be helped to sit up when the time comes. It carries the relaxation over into sitting, standing and then moving.

One last point. As you do this delightful exer-cise you will notice that to give a massage is in itself a relaxing and nurturing experience. Then to re-ceive one will be just an added bonus.

Finish with tea and cookies, just spending some quiet time with your friends. You will all feel a deeper level of connection; a wonderful nonverbal relating will have happened which brings people closer together.

■ TRAIN MASSAGE

This exercise is a variation of the octopus that can be done easily anywhere – at the beach, at a party, any place where a group of friends gather. It can be done on the floor, in chairs or even standing. The idea is to tune into both giving and receiving, to relax under the hands of the person behind you while transmitting to the person in front of you, through your hands, the message to relax.

To make it fair, after five to ten minutes the per-son in front should rotate to the back of the line.

TRANSFORMING TENSION

In the first secret of living in balance we discussed starting from where you are – acknowledging yourself as you really are and being honest with yourself. Now we would like you to develop this one step further.

Everyone has aspirations, dreams and desires. Whatever these goals may be, however silly or unrealistic, they are a part of you and should be acknowledged. Through creatively transforming tension dreams can come true. Here's a simple example of how it works.

A doctor friend of mine was afraid of dogs. He used to get nervous and agitated around them, and the dogs picked up on his fear and as a result

he had several nasty incidences. He played at being brave and fearless around dogs but it did not change anything, the dogs always managed to pick-up on his fears anyway. Then he tried transforming tension. He simply acknowledged to himself, as well as to his friends, that, yes, he was afraid of dogs, and that he would like to be relaxed and friendly with them. He set up in his mind both these ideas: on the one hand, how he truly is, and on the other hand, how he would like to be. Between these two points there exists a tension.

Tension is an energy. When held in and not expressed it can cause a great deal of discomfort in the body-mind. When, however, the tension is

given a form and allowed to be recognized for what it is, it can move towards a resolution. This is the creative use of tension.

My friend did nothing more than acknowledge his situation. He just kept on reminding himself of the truth of it. Then one day he met a dog that seemed as mean as could be, and just as he expected, he immediately felt afraid. But something else was also present: his wish not to be scared. He actually started talking to the dog, telling him the story out loud. Perhaps it was the very sound of his voice that made the difference. The voice was a bit shaky but not nearly as bad as he had imagined it, and the animal liked his voice. Soon he was singing to the dog, who in turn was wagging his tail to the music. The doctor ended up petting the dog and walking away from a minor miracle.

Our dreams are often in conflict with our reality and so usually remain as dreams. We don't give them the attention they need to make them come true. Either that or we get so caught up in trying to realize them that we cannot enjoy it when we do get what we want. For example, we dream of making money so that we can travel, but the very act of making money becomes so important in itself that the journey we have dreamed about gets repeatedly postponed in favor of the job that will bring us more money. By relaxing into accepting who you are and what you wish for yourself, you give your dreams enough space to actually come about.

In transforming tension, the important thing is not to limit yourself to any one particular way of making your dream come true. Instead you hold your dream in suspension while being aware of how far you are from realizing it. Trusting in that gap allows some unexpected creative way for your dream to manifest, to occur. For example, one friend who left her husband eight years ago, has always claimed she hated living alone, yet she continues to live alone because she had limited her dream to the perfect companion. If she were able to make a true and honest appraisal of where she is in her life, and what her dream, taken down to the bare essentials, actually turns out to be, she could open herself to the possibility of sharing her home with one or several people, whoever they are, and go on from there. By living with others she would be less lonely and meet more people, and she would be giving herself more of a chance to meet someone closer to her ideal. At least the first step of her dream would have been taken.

By taking the first step, the dreams evolve in themselves; we often find that the details of what we thought we wanted turn out to be quite different when actually lived out.

Start by looking at your most simple and immediately available wants: You've always wanted to try that chocolate cake at the nearby pastry shop but never allowed yourself. Or you've longed to see the sun rise in the morning but haven't quite made it. You can think about it but it'll remain a dream. Or you can acknowledge that you would like to eat cake but rationalize that you're too fat. Or you can buy the cake and eat it consciously and discover you only want two bites and never hunger for it again. Likewise you may acknowledge your desire to see the sun rise but rationalize that basically you are not a morning person. Or you can set your alarm and see what happens.

Your ideas about yourself (as too fat for chocolate cake, or not a morning person) were shaped in your past. Your dream to eat cake or see the sun rise are in the future. These are the two polarities between which you establish a dynamic tension. Both polarities are in a sense dreams because what we call reality only exists in the present moment, somewhere between the two. It is the only place where all things happen, the land where dreams can come true. When we begin to transform tension to manifest small and immediately accessible things, we can build up an experience of it working that gives us confidence for the bigger things. Who knows that yacht you've always wanted may soon be yours.

These guys don't even need to squeeze to relax.

■ SQUEEZE AND RELAX

The most maddening invitation ever extended my way was when I was lying on the chiropractor's table twisted up like a pretzel, fully aware that a colossal manipulation of my body was about to take place, and there was this huge brute of a man hovering over me saying sweetly, " Now this won't hurt a bit – take a deep breath and relax! "

Of course we all know that if there were no danger of hurt at all, my chiropractor wouldn't even mention the word. Furthermore, if I were able on command to just relax, then my body would never have become so out of line in the first place and I wouldn't be lying on his table paying the price.

One way of relating to tension is to see it as contained energy; energy that wants to express itself but for some reason has not had the chance to do so. Under these circumstances the energy cannot loosen, and cannot expel itself. Instead it tightens and solidifies, and goes inwards. By paying attention to it we allow it to fulfill its aim, and to move and shift. The natural outcome of this movement is relaxation.

When we ignore tension we fail to do our bodies justice. Tension is as valid an expression of malfunction as is a cramp or a bleeding wound. The difference is that we can forget about tension and still manage our lives – tricky with a bleeding wound. We may forget about it, but like with any other illness, tension does not go away by being ignored. Slowly, slowly, it creates recurrent discomfort until it leads to acute and manifestly more debilitating sicknesses.

This is also true when we try to fight it. Tension has a paradoxical way of goading us to be rid of it by making us strain and demand more of ourselves when what we really need is to do the reverse and rest. We've been up since dawn, taken the kids to school, spent hours at the supermarket, run around the office, and had lunch with a belligerent client. We've carted our aged parent to the clinic, and cooked dinner for an equally overworked family only to run off to an evening at the theater and a late nightcap at the end of it all.

Suppressing tension by the regular intake of drugs or alcohol could well be the most dangerous form of coping with this powerhouse of distress. The effects of extreme drug abuse are well enough documented in other sources and do not need our analysis here. But it is worth bearing in mind how even the slow continuous excessive use of stimulants and sedatives – those that we take for granted in our daily lives – form a cycle of dependency that becomes more and more of a burden to break.

Tension is the main symptom of that most familiar malaise of the modern world: stress. It functions as a warning signal – a request for your help. There is no need to either ignore, fight or suppress it. Understanding that a small amount is natural in our day-to-day life and can actually stimulate us into fresh beginnings is a good way to start.

This section is about identifying and responding to stress early in the process. The following exercise works on the simple principle of acknowledging the tensions in your body, recognizing and actually recreating them by exaggerating them. This can have a miraculous effect. By giving your body permission to be tense, you are also allowing it to be otherwise.

Two of you can experiment with this exercise, taking turns to read the instructions to the other. Or you can do it alone. Understanding both the exercise and the basic principle behind it will help in your day-to-day life. Honor your tension. It's pointing a finger somewhere.

Pick a quiet dark room and lie on a firm but not hard surface. If possible lie on some pleasingly tactile texture, perhaps silk or satin. Lie on your back, making sure your body is fully supported and take two or three deep breaths.

Say to yourself either quietly or out loud: "Right now in my body there are certain tensions, which I accept as part of myself at this moment. I understand that they are merely energies that are held within me waiting for expression. I will now explore them and allow them to move."

Take a couple more deep breaths remembering to exhale as fully as you inhale.

Now curl just your toes towards the ground with some effort but no real strain. Hold to the count of five and let go. Next arch the toes up towards your head. Hold to the count of five and let go. Repeat curling the toes down, this time letting the whole foot go down with it. Hold to the count of five and let go. Curl the toes up towards your head and let the foot follow, tensing upwards. Hold to the count of five and let go.

Back to the toes and the foot, curling down, this time feeling the calf muscle getting tight and short as it pulls the foot. Hold to the count of five and let go. Again, curl up the toes and the foot, feeling the calf muscles getting tense from being lengthened and stretched. Hold to the count of five and let go.

You are starting to get the feel of the exercise. Be aware that you are not overdoing it and straining your body unnecessarily, yet put enough effort into it so that you're really feeling the part of the

Squeezed and relaxed.

Everything is flowing again.

body you are working on. If you're unsure, use less effort at first and build it up slowly.

Now curl the toes and foot down, this time letting the knee area get tense. Hold to the count of five and release. Repeat this curling upwards, again paying attention to the knee area getting tight. Hold to the count of five and let go.

Once more, feet down and tighten the thigh muscles. Hold, count five and release. Now feet up; thighs tight. Hold, count and let go.

Now press the knees together, pushing them against each other.

Push, hold to five and let go.

Next, squeeze your buttocks and pelvic muscles together, drawing the buttocks both in and up. Hold the position, count to five and return to normal.

Turn both legs sideways so the toes move away from each other as far as possible. Hold and release.

Now tense up the whole of your leg any way you want, and hold your breath. This time hold the position for as long as you can hold your breath. When you let go, rest for a few moments allowing your legs to get heavy on the ground. Feel the weight of them while they are relaxing.

After a short break, carry on by pushing the small of your back into the ground while your pelvis tilts upwards. Hold to a count of five and let go.

Proceed up your spine pushing a different part of the back downwards, and hold to a count of five. Repeat four to six times until you have worked all the way up to the top of the neck.

Next, focus on the area of your ribs, diaphragm, chest and lungs. Breathe in deep and hold the breath. The amount of time will vary with the individual, but hold as long as you can without over-straining. When you breath out, let the air go – don't push it. Just open the throat, and allow the air to rush out by itself as it would from a deflating balloon. Repeat with the breath once more.

Now clench your fingers, palms and whole hands, and hold it like that counting to five. Now let go. Bend your wrists and elbows. Tense; hold and release.

Pull your shoulders up as close to your ears as possible. Hold; count to five; release. Bring your shoulders up again, this time curling them forwards into the front of your chest. Hold, count, and let them down.

Focus on your neck and throat, and swallow forcefully a few times letting the throat tighten. Then release. Shut your eyes tight and squeeze to the count of five. Twitch your nose. Raise your eyebrows and feel the creases in your forehead. Close your eyes tight, twitch your nose, raise your eyebrows, and tighten your face and neck all at once. Hold and relax.

Repeat the above letting the back of your neck tighten as well. If sounds come out during this part of the exercise – groans or whatever – encourage them.

Now take a few more deep breaths using less and less effort each time. Let your whole body relax and get heavier. As the force of gravity pulls you more and more towards the floor, feel yourself sinking and allow yourself to go on sinking.

This is the end of the formal part of the exercise. It is now up to you to respond to the wishes of your body. You may drift off to sleep or feel like getting up and dancing, but having tuned into the energies circulating in your system, stay with them and do whatever feels right – there are no shoulds at this time.

If you do this technique on a regular basis you will find it takes only fifteen minutes; give yourself a bit longer for maximum flexibility at the end. You will also find that it is a valuable form of exercise: good for muscle tone and beneficial to the blood circulation and especially to the lymphatic fluids which move through the body when the muscles are contracting and elongating.

■ PAIN

We give pain a hard time – trying to get rid of it

with drugs, dulling it with alcohol, and distracting ourselves from it by any means that we can. This is because pain hurts.

Yet pain serves a natural and significant role in protecting us. When we casually place our hand on a hot stove we receive immediate signals to remove our hand before damage is done. This signal comes in the form of pain. When the pain persists, it is another message to us that some harm has been done to the body and that steps should be taken to treat the burn. These are obvious yet important messages that the brain is sending to us. These messages we usually heed and there is no problem.

Problems do, however, begin to arise when we start treating this ally in strange ways. Very early conditioning, from a time when we were unable to help ourselves and depended on others, makes us afraid of pain. We fear that pain will come and that we will not be able to do anything to alleviate it when it does. This fear leads us into putting a lot of energy and effort into avoiding it. Unfortunately, avoidance only leads to greater and greater pain. For pain always has a message. If we avoid hearing the message, or if we hear but we ignore the pain, then the pain has to turn up the volume in order to be heard.

If the fear of pain does not lead to avoidance or to ignoring pain, it might then lead to constantly anticipating pain. When we anticipate the hurt we tighten and constrict ourselves in order to prepare for it, which then makes the pain more painful. Then we think, "I knew it was going to hurt," and tighten even more. So it hurts more, and so on.

We can react to pain, and even to the fear of pain, so strongly that we deaden ourselves to such a degree that we no longer feel it at all. The outcome of this, though, is that we no longer feel anything else either. Often it happens during a series of body-work sessions that parts of the body begin to hurt that were not hurting before. The body is waking up from a nearly dead state, and the first sensations to arise are the ones that had been cut

off a long time ago. Soon, however, the aches and pains go, and a new feeling of liveliness that the person had just about forgotten existed comes into being.

All of the above strategies – avoiding, anticipating, ignoring – are inappropriate responses to pain. The very first thing that we have to realize is that we are no longer helpless babies at the mercy of others. We can act, we can take steps to minimize unnecessary pain, and we can respond to necessary pain in an appropriate fashion.

Once we clearly see this point we can begin to make friends with pain and to use it as an ally. We can even transform pain into pleasure.

One of the definitions of pain is resistance to change – a sometimes necessary resistance. A hand on the stove implies change. If left there, the hand will become a damaged and useless appendage. We are right to resist this kind of change. But if our response is to continuously try to resist change, then pain will be in our lives to an extreme degree. Resistance leads to fight, to a desperate holding-on, and to a constriction of great proportion.

When an infant moves, that very movement is pleasurable. When it laughs, even when it cries sometimes, the actual act is pleasurable. For pleasure is unrestricted movement of energy. As energy moves outwards, pleasure is created. But stop that infant from doing something, restrict the completion of the movement, and pain arises. The movement towards completion is stopped, and the resulting holding of the energy eventually produces pain. As we grow, this pain becomes chronic and is with us most of the time. We structure our lives to constantly repeat situations in which the same thing happens, as if to give us the opportunity to complete the movement of energy. Except now our fear of the pain we know we have felt in the past means it is us stopping ourselves, creating our own pain.

For example, during deep body therapy sessions people often contact very painful areas within their bodies. When the pain is acknowledged, felt and released, perhaps through crying, people invariably report that they feel pleasure in the same place where only moments before there was pain. When the energy is allowed to move and when the resistance is dropped, there is an immediate shift. The pain turns to pleasure. This is the process of letting go.

A story: an extremely rich Bombay businessman came to one of our body therapy clinics that we held in India some years back. His complaint was a chronic crippling pain in his back. For years he had traveled to doctors, clinics and spas all over the world to ease his suffering. X-rays, probes and tests had found nothing of a structural nature to be wrong. Yet the pain was very much there. Furthermore, because he had already received so many therapies without success, he had developed a fatalistic attitude, feeling that this pain would haunt him the rest of his life. This man was coming to us simply out of habit. Deep down he was convinced that nothing could be done to alleviate his suffering. Yet within a fortnight all the pain had miraculously disappeared, and it has not returned to this day. This is how it happened.

During the first session the businessman could hardly allow the Rebalancer (the body therapist) to even touch his back. Instead, the chest area and the legs were worked upon. The therapist sensed that his client was holding onto his pain on a very deep level. The muscles in the spinal region seemed traumatized, as if grasping or holding on with all their might. When questioned as to the exact time the pain had first manifested itself, the man reported that he could not quite remember.

During the next two sessions therapist and client played a kind of cat-and-mouse game, the therapist trying different approaches to be able to work directly on the afflicted area, and the client, ever wary, trying to avoid this contact. Still, he was beginning to trust and relax under the skillful hands and gentle encouragement of the Rebalancer.

Halfway through the fourth session, as the therapist worked he began to relate a very funny and risque anecdote to the Bombay businessman whose attention was completely held by the story. At one point, the therapist casually placed his hand on the traumatized area while continuing talking. Gradually, casually and very gently he began to work on it. By the time the businessman realized what had happened the therapist had been working on the area for some minutes. Through a combination of humor and trust a certain relaxation had happened and an opening was created. The stage was set for change to occur.

When the businessman arrived for his next session, there was a glimmer of excitement in his eyes, which had always before been rather forlorn looking. This time the therapist went straight to the danger zone and began working there slowly and softly. The client was noticeably more cooperative and less fearfully protective of his back. The therapist began to apply more pressure penetrating deeper and deeper into the muscles surrounding the spine. Tears began to well up in the man's eyes, which suddenly turned to uncontrollable sobbing and wailing.

Forty-five minutes later, a radiant man told his story. Years before, his wife had died. At the funeral he had been unable to cry. In fact, a part of him had felt happy to be a free man again (in India divorce is still very uncommon). So strong was his guilt about this feeling that quite unconsciously he had begun to punish himself for his evil thoughts. He had even managed to forget that the pain had begun right at this time.

The very tissue of our bodies has a cellular memory which can record and recall pain and pleasure. His pain was held deep within the musculature of his back. When contacted by the skilled hands of the body-worker the trapped memory was released and re-lived. At this time, however, he not only felt his guilt, but was able to experience the genuine grief that he had felt at the death of his wife, but which at the time had gotten muddled up

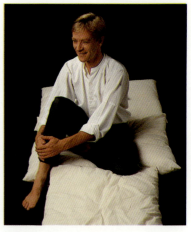

1 Pain makes us contract, tighten and withdraw from the world.

2 By acknowledging the pain we take the first step towards releasing it.

3 Feeling better! But take it easy, have a cup of tea. Do what feels right.

with other emotions that he was trying to suppress.

This kind of story is by no means unusual. It happens all the time. Most of us spend much effort either trying to avoid pains, or, if you are from the no-pain-no-gain school of thought, in enduring greater and lesser pains. This is an unnecessary waste of time and energy.

We must all learn to pay attention to the signals that our bodies are constantly transmitting, and if we begin by paying attention, we can nip any problems in the bud. If we miss the earliest signals we can still try to correct situations and relieve pain quickly. This is a way of life that should be taught at an early age. It is called preventive medicine. Just as modern dentistry has developed preventive measures, so too modern medicine will one day (hopefully very soon) develop its preventive measures. It has of course already begun, in recommending healthy diets and active lifestyles, but it could go much further. Then our children will

know radiant health and well-being. And no doubt a cornerstone of the new medicine will be each and every one of us listening to our own body and its messages.

Even today, for those of us who have not been taught correctly it is not too late to tune in. It takes only a little willingness to innovate and to take the time. We must all become experts, specialists of ourselves. We must take back our personal power and reassume responsibility for our bodies. Not as a difficult burden to be shouldered, not as yet another chore in our busy lives, but rather as an exciting challenge in knowing ourselves and in reaching our true potential. It is an adventure that we are talking about. An adventure that includes our whole beings – body, mind, heart and soul.

Different personalities respond in vastly different ways to situations. Some people can cope with difficulties much better than others. For them difficulties are challenges and ways of growing stronger, and it seems that some struggle and pain

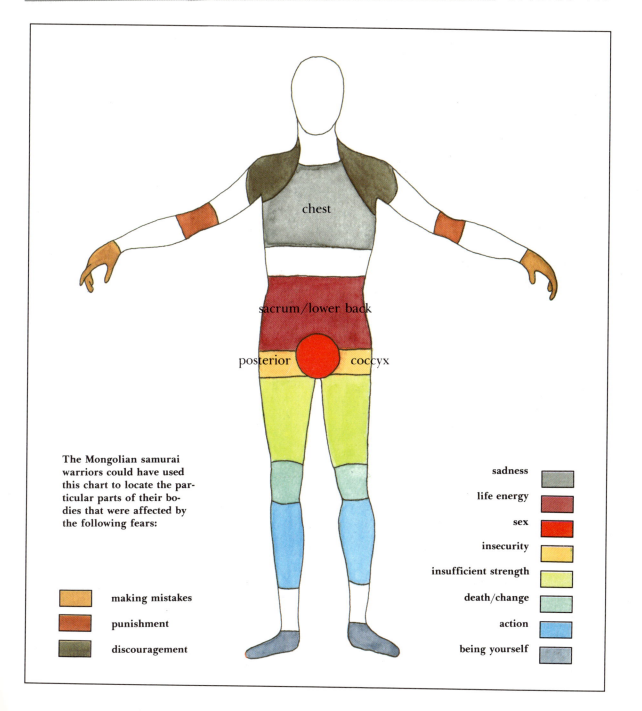

chest

sacrum/lower back

posterior   coccyx

The Mongolian samurai warriors could have used this chart to locate the particular parts of their bodies that were affected by the following fears:

making mistakes

punishment

discouragement

sadness

life energy

sex

insecurity

insufficient strength

death/change

action

being yourself

is actually beneficial and intrinsic to personal development. And the human body has amazing powers of adapting and coping with different situations and of healing itself.

In this book we are using the most simple techniques available to slightly alter the course of our lives. There is a reason for this approach. We are learning through the small details that it is actually within the realm of possibility to create new choices during the course of our daily lives and in very simple situations.

When we are stuck in a snow bank it is no use to gun the engine and try to break out by sheer force. The tires only spin and we sink deeper and deeper into a hole. A much better approach is to slowly rock the car back and forth thereby building up some momentum. When the momentum reaches a certain level the car suddenly pops out of the snow bank and we are free! This approach requires patience and a relaxed attitude, combined with small changes, the gentle back-and-forth rocking that slowly increases allowing the necessary momentum to be developed.

We all look for sudden change, instantaneous transformations, and radical and dramatic alterations in our lives. As we get older we become resigned to our fate, no longer expecting any change. Both of these attitudes are lacking something. That something is a continuous yet soft momentum, and an openness and welcoming of change in the little things in life, which gives us the momentum to move through the more dramatic situations we encounter with grace, enthusiasm and all of our faculties available to get the best out of each situation.

Try this simple exercise next time you have a headache or any minor pain. Instead of immediately rushing to the medicine cabinet for aspirin, take a little time out for yourself. Take the phone off the hook, and otherwise make sure you have some undisturbed space. Go to a place where you feel most comfortable. Maybe put on some soft music. Loosen any tight clothing and get into a comfortable position. Begin by paying attention to your breath. Without trying to change anything about it just feel the quality of your breath. Is it deep or shallow? Fast or slow? In your throat, chest or belly, or a combination of places? Remember, you are not trying to change anything about it, just noticing it. The interesting thing that will happen very quickly is that all by itself the breath will begin to change. It may get fuller, deeper or more relaxed. Or, just as likely, it will get more agitated, shallow and fast. It doesn't matter. After a few minutes with the breath take notice of the whole body. Is it really in a relaxed position, or does it want a change: to lie down, to sit up, to wiggle and stretch, to stand up and shake, to pace, or to be very still. Cooperate, listen and let the body do what it wants.

When you have established what the body wants, move on to the next stage. Allow your mind to locate the exact spot in the body that seems to be the center of the pain. Go right into the pain. Let your hand rest on top of the area. Let your breath come right into the painful area. It's true: you can breathe into any spot in your body, so breathe right into the pain. With your mind, try to feel it. Describe it to yourself: the shape, color, size, type of pain. Throbbing, deep, dull, intense, diffuse – pains do have very different qualities. Again, just be with the pain without trying to change anything. You are just noticing it as deeply as possible, feeling it in as many ways as you can. Develop your own technique.

You don't have to do everything at once. This is not a skill-testing exercise. See what way helps you get the most familiar with the pain. Don't be surprised if it very quickly begins to change. If it moves to another spot or changes in size or disappears entirely. Just hang out with it as fully and totally as you can for as long a time as it feels comfortable. If emotions come up, or distracting thoughts, let them. The purpose of this exercise is to practice reading the messages pain is sending to you.

It is nice to end the exercise by a few minutes of doing nothing in particular. Whatever you feel like doing. If you have dozed off, good. If you feel tense or emotional afterwards, allow that to be there as well. The body is telling you something, but it may take some time to tune in, especially if the message is unpleasant. Even unpleasant messages are better than trying to tune out the pain or carrying it around with you like a burden.

There need be no pains or aches. You can do it in a preventative way to catch them even before they fully arise. This kind of preventative measure helps return you even quicker to a state of natural balance.

The practice of *chua ka* derives from the Mongolian samurai warriors of 2000 years ago who claimed that bodies hold the memories of every physical pain they have experienced. After each of their battles they ritualistically massaged themselves with pieces of ivory that went deep into the musculature to release the fear accumulated during the fight. This practice was based on the connections between particular fears and the parts of the body (see chart).

When fear is allowed to surface it is given the opportunity to complete itself – to be released. If the fear is held inside, it is made into a vicious circle that leads to distortions in the physical emotional make-up.

Pain is fear of an emotion stored in the body, not the emotion itself. Pain is therefore a feeling that is afraid to express itself, to move. For example, sadness in itself can be a very deep feeling that gives depth and another dimension to our being. As such it can be enjoyed in its pure form just as a baby can enjoy the release of energy when it cries.

However, when the fear of sadness is in the chest and will not express itself, any activity such as deep breathing, triggers the fear and we deal with it by avoiding deep breath and holding the breath instead.

There is no need to actually express the pain (i.e. cry). It is only that the space for its expression is created, if permission is somehow granted.

The result is that our chest is in contraction (caved in, as in defeat) or held in expansion (puffed out, as with a tough-guy) and our range of choices is unconsciously inhibited. We may take the stance of happy-go-lucky tough-guy, but always be a sad person.

So it is not really sadness as such but fear of sadness that leads to lack of choices. That fear went into the chest at a time of life, probably early on in childhood, when we didn't know how to appropriately deal with it.

Fritz Perls has said that pain is your opinion of a sensation or experience. In a session, someone in great pain, by calling it pain, may change his attitude and see it as something, in which case it ceases to be pain. Look at pain that isn't actually damaging us, for example, the hurt made by the body-worker's manipulations, and you will see what is meant by this.

■ PLEASURE

It is not surprising that most of us have some difficulties in relating to pain. What does come as a surprise is our basic inability to relate totally to pleasure. Perhaps it is because each is but one side of the same coin that our response to pleasure, our pleasure capacity, is limited. For example, worry about cancer will limit our enjoyment of a cigarette. Yet, if we continue to smoke without fully enjoying each cigarette, we will smoke more, thereby increasing the harmful effects while deceasing the pleasures. The same is true for alcohol, food, sex, and all the little pleasures of life.

When we were young we knew how to enjoy our pleasures much more. Observing a kid with a huge triple decker ice-cream we see a totality of enjoyment bordering the ecstatic. As we grow older and more sophisticated we hold back from the enjoyment of pleasures to their fullness, as if we did not

Some societies try to eliminate both pain and pleasure.

really deserve to be enjoying ourselves as much as possible. Society seems to be afraid of too much pleasure, reasoning that a person who is fully enjoying will be a less functioning member of society. To some extent this may be true. Those that are already enjoying life will be less competitive, less aggressive, and probably less controllable. They may be having too much fun to fight in wars and run around killing one another. The hippie movement of the late sixties with its slogan of "make love not war" was trying to move towards a lifestyle of accepting and maximizing pleasure. In their idealistic approach they may have perhaps swung too much to one extreme, into hedonism, yet in some ways they were on the right track. Life in its totality provides us with both pain and pleasure. We cannot afford to deny either aspect but rather make the most of both sides of the coin.

There have been throughout history countless philosophies that have glamorized either pain or pleasure. And there have been societies that have tried to eliminate both. The mystics throughout the ages have used a different approach. Their way has been to accept and experience whatever comes in its totality, and through that totalness to reach a point of understanding wherein pain and pleasure are kept in balance. The mystics maintain that it is neither pain nor pleasure but rather attachment that is the problem. We want to avoid pain and we seek pleasure. Avoiding, we push parts of life away and, holding on, we kill another part. We want the pleasure, we don't want pain, and that's fair enough, but life is not always fair. We don't always get what we want; and then our attachment, our desire to gain pleasures, and our desire to avoid pain cause great problems. The end result is an inability to relate properly to either issue.

In this exercise we ask you to do something simple that gives you pleasure. Whether it be in eating, drinking, sports, or just having a leisurely bath or a nap, it's up to you. For now choose something rather simple and immediate that you can do alone. The object of the exercise is to be so totally in the pleasure, so lost in it with no other issues entering the scene that when you are finished you feel totally satisfied. The more total we can manage to be in pleasure the less room there is for any attachment coming into it. Thus we do not want to cling to it, so when it is finished it is truly completed.

If you are at a loss as to how to proceed, observe

Others focus only on the pleasure.

a child for a while, playing, totally absorbed in what they are doing. So absorbed, that when something new comes along they have no need to cling or get attached to the old. They are ready to move on to something new.

Engage in the pleasurable activity of your choice in exactly the same way. Allow no guilt, criticism, judgment or morality to enter in. Be absorbed in pleasure. Start with something easy for you, that you know you can really get a lot of pleasure from. Practice totality, and let it spread more and more into the very fabric of your life. Give yourself the permission to enjoy the pleasures of life as much as you did when you were an innocent child. You will be pleasantly surprised that everyday activities become more and more fun and the amount of pleasure in your life increases without any effort on your part.

DIS-EASE

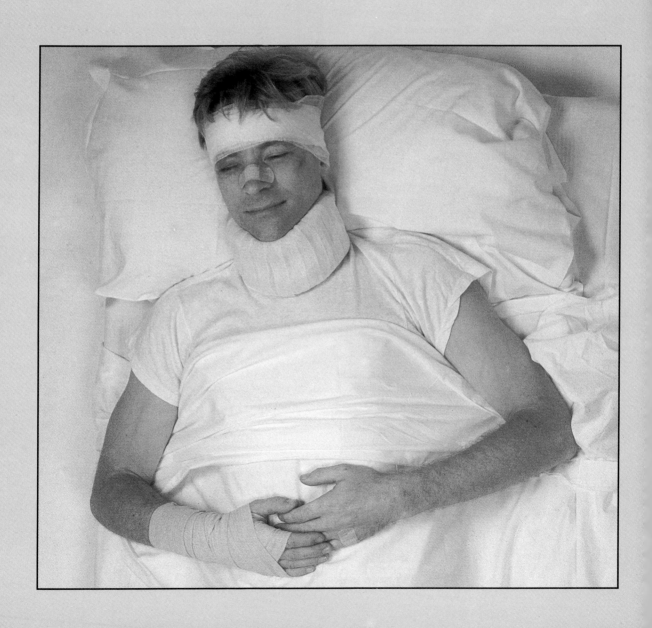

In his now classic book *Anatomy of an Illness* (W.W. Norton Co, N.Y. London, 1979) Norman Cousins describes an illness that doctors said he had only a one in 500 chance of recovering from.

Rather than accepting the doctors' grim verdict he took responsibility for himself. He found a doctor that he could work together with, moved out of the hospital where he did not enjoy the food or the mood of the place and into a hotel room. He experimented with different healing techniques, some quite unorthodox, such as watching funny movies. He found that genuine laughter gives relief from pain. By taking action he took himself out of the downward spiral of fear, depression and panic that accompanies severe diseases and constructed his own uplifting spiral of acceptance, action and self help that eventually brought about a complete and to some peoples' eyes a miraculous cure.

All of us at times fall ill, or into a state of disease. Whether the malady is serious or minor there is a number of aspects that are helpful to recognize and to act upon. Every state of dis-ease, even those caused by apparent accidents are signals from the body-mind (from ourselves to ourselves). Probably the message has been coming for some time now but we have ignored it until it gets serious enough that we can no longer ignore it. One frequently sent but often ignored message is slow down. Others might be: too much stress, overeating, fear, loneliness, disappointment, and on and on. Dis-ease is a lack of ease within oneself. What is creating this state. If your body is trying to tell you something be courteous enough to listen and accept the message. Not only is the message something that needs to be fed, but the very act of listening brings us into closer harmony with our bodies with ourselves. When there is harmony there is more relaxation, more ease in life and less dis-ease.

Along with listening to the body goes taking care of it in the most appropriate way possible.

Modern western medicine administered by a doctor you trust is a powerful and effective tool in many cases. However there is a wide assortment of approaches within the healing arts that are also valid and in some cases very effective. Holistic medicine, homeopathy, acupuncture, herbs, diets, fasting, physiotherapy, and massage are only a few of the many possibilities. Different methods fit for different ailments. Experiment and find out what works best for you.

Our bodies have great recuperative powers. Sometimes we hinder our own healing process by giving away all our power to physicians. They know a lot and their expertise is needed, but sometimes we are the best experts on ourselves. There needs to be a balance between empowering our doctor and empowering our own inner healing agencies.

A third factor to remember is that of self-acceptance. When you are sick in bed make the most of it. It's no use giving oneself a hard time about being sick. Once it has happened we may as well enjoy it, accept that this is our condition at this moment, and make the best of it. Nothing assists the healing process as much as good spirits. Yet many of us aggravate our dis-ease with guilt ("I should have been more careful," "Now what have I done?" "If only..."). Accept yourself as you are in this moment and well being is not far away. Enjoy the time spent in bed. Pamper yourself. Give yourself lots of attention and let others fuss over you as well. Any ailment is always a sign that we need to give ourselves some attention, so give it freely and generously. You will appreciate it.

That's our three–fold plan for living in balance through ill health. Listen to the messages of your body-mind. Do what you can to get back to health, while at the same time accepting and enjoying the benefits of dis-ease. In this way we take full responsibility for ourselves, on the physical, mental and emotional levels. We know we are doing the best that we can in transforming dis-ease into at-ease.

■ FREE DANCE

Free dance has no special moves or steps. It is simply an expression of your energy, a response to the present moment that moves and changes with the moment. So, pull the shades, kick off your shoes, crank up the sound, and let her rip!

Free dance is wild and wonderful, slow and sensual, frantic and frivolous. Free dance is simply you in all of your varied moods able to shift from one mood to another and swing from one extreme to its polar opposite at a moment's notice.

Often, during the course of a normal day, we experience many feelings and emotions that are not appropriate to express at that time. We tend to store these and allow them to build up, to fill us up until we are ready to explode. Free dance is a conscious explosion. A creative rather than destructive way of letting go of excess energy, pent up emotions, and the pressures from using the mind too much. Free dance is even a way of recharging our depleted energy and getting moving again. Physically healthy and good exercise, mentally relaxing and emotionally expressive, free dance is easy and fun. What more can you ask for? Perhaps a dancing partner. But when you're happily dancing that too is bound to come along, attracted by the energy of your unique free dance.

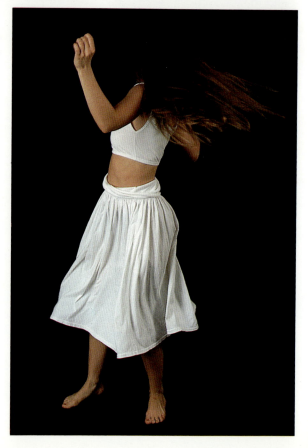

BEDTIME

SLIPPING INTO SLEEP

■ I AM WHAT I AM AND I LIKE IT

Affirmations, visualizations, and self-hypnosis have become a very popular field of exploration these days in all New Age circles. On the most simple level these practices engage in us talking to ourselves in a positive and creative fashion. Psychiatrists, psychologists and researchers have found that there are vast layers of the mind that lie beneath the conscious mind that we are familiar with. They talk of the subconscious, unconscious, even the collective unconscious, and the image they use is that of an iceberg, where the visible part that is above the water is only a small portion, maybe one–tenth while the main mass of the iceberg is hidden under water. The conscious is the visible layer, while our unconscious lies hidden and yet has a great effect upon our life. The unconscious is like a vast and complex computer with the ability to store incredible amounts of information. Scientists speculate that the unconscious has stored every experience and every moment of our lives, and perhaps even has access to the collective computer of all mankind. In any case, through the creative use of our imaginations we can begin to program this vast computer in a way that is more beneficial to our lives. Much of what has gone in is random and haphazard ideas; most of it registered at a very early age when our survival was the most important issue and our real understanding was not yet formed. As a result, many of the programs in the computer are outdated and ineffective. Yet they remain in the unconscious from where they exert a strong influence upon our lives. For example, during some de-hypnotherapy sessions I was able to trace a recurring physical ailment, a digestive disorder, back to a very early life experience. As a baby I had learned that in order to survive in a world where I was basically helpless and at the mercy of others it was helpful to be able to cry very loudly. I learned to cry loudly by contracting my guts in a certain way. Thirty–eight years later, no longer helpless and dependent on others, I still contracted my intestinal walls to get attention. Once I was able to see this pattern I could explain to my unconscious that this behavior was no longer appropriate and suggest some new ways of being. Over time I was able to put a new tape into the computer: one that allowed my life to function better.

Much good literature as well as courses are already available in this field, so we will not go into it here in any more detail. But we do recognize the potential we all have for improving the quality of our life through the power of our own imagination. At the core of the whole process we feel is the theme of self-acceptance. If we are constantly trying to change ourselves because of an inner dissatisfaction we get involved in an endless torturous path where we are never good enough, never satisfied and never truly relaxed. By all means change is one of the basic laws of life, and as long as we do change, we might as well have some say in the process and move more into the directions that we enjoy. But let us remember, a rose, is a rose, is a rose. As we are right now we are all unique and complete human beings. A rose does not want to be a lotus, or a tree. It accepts and lives itself fully as it is. Of course there is always room to grow and evolve, but if we can relax and enjoy ourselves right here and right now then positive growth is bound to happen on its own. So by all means, hypnotize, actualize, visualize, affirm and do whatever you will, but realize, too, that right here and now you are already it.

■ GOOD HABITS

Good habits are the rituals that we engage in. More specifically we are referring to those rituals that produce a certain state of mind, whether it be excitement, concentration, or in this case a state of relaxation which is desirable before going to sleep at night.

Especially after a hectic or stressful day we need to take time to unwind from the pressures of the day in order to sleep well and allow the body-mind to fully rejuvenate during the night and be ready and fresh for the next day.

Different people employ varied means to prepare for sleep. Some like to take the dog for a walk, while others enjoy a leisurely hot bath, perhaps with scented oils in the water, by candle light and with a glass of wine. Yet others prefer to curl up with a good book and a glass of milk or camomile tea. Some people like to do some slow stretching exercises or some self massage or even massage with a partner. Certainly, judging by the soothing effects touch and massage has on crying babies this technique works well.

Women seem to have more night time rituals in the form of creams and lotions to be applied to the body. Both sexes make lists of things to remember for the next day in order to clean the mind of potential worries that may keep us awake. Some people have peculiar habits that they must do in order to be able to sleep, such as pulling the curtains right to let no light in or arranging the covers a certain way, and so on.

The underlying wisdom of these habits is to send clear signals to the body-mind that sleep time is on its way. If you are a person who has trouble getting to sleep at night you would do well to adopt some pleasant rituals and to do them repeatedly in order to signal to your system that sleep is on the way. The backward review of the day is a very effective way of quieting the mind, of unwinding from the day, and of moving into a relaxing sleep.

Studies done with insomniacs have shown that the very fear of not being able to sleep keeps people awake. If you are troubled with insomnia the most important part to remember is to simply accept the fact that you cannot sleep without anxiety. Worrying that you must be fresh for the morning only serves to create a tension that produces the opposite effect. If you are unable to sleep, allow that state to be there, use the time creatively. Try meditating or reading a good book or simply lie still, focus on your breathing, and do one of the relaxation exercises outlined in this book. And remember, whatever you do, do it for its own sake and enjoy it for itself, not as a means to get to sleep. You may well fall asleep, but if you're trying hard to do it tension is created and a tense mind cannot fall asleep. In a way we must trick ourselves into relaxation by accepting and enjoying our state of tension. If you allow the tension to be there with no struggle, the pendulum swings into the opposite polarity of relaxation. If we worry about our tension we hold on to it and actually exaggerate it, creating a vicious circle of increasing insomnia.

Even if you stay up late and only get four or five hours sleep it may well be enough for you if those few hours of sleep are deep and restful. This may well be more effective than resorting to sleeping pills which give more hours of sleep but of a poorer quality. For sleeping tablets put us into a drugged state that is chemically induced and not in keeping with our natural rhythms. It is a kind of forced sleep from which we awake groggy, disoriented and not truly rested.

In some cases a sleeping pill may be beneficial but not on an everyday basis where the pill becomes our habit. Better to create good habits that are our own rituals to take us into the realm of sleep. Tests have been conducted where insomniacs were told they were getting sleeping pills and were given placebos, simple sugar tablets with no chemicals in them. Yet the placebos worked because the people thought they were going to sleep from the tablets and were able then to relax and to actually sleep. The placebo lulled the mind and body into a relaxed state, and we can do the same with our nightly rituals. Happy Dreams!

■ RERUN AND UNWIND

This exercise has many immediate benefits. For people who have difficulty falling asleep at night it acts as a natural sleeping pill. For those troubled by the events of the day it provides a new perspective from which to view their actions. And for those of us who are interested in becoming more conscious in our daily lives, repeated practice of this technique brings new awareness and insight into our patterns, habits, rhythms, and into the very core of our ways of functioning.

Once you are comfortable in bed and have nothing more to attend to, you are ready to experiment with this method. The idea is to run through in your mind everything that has happened during the course of your day. The tricky part is that you must go backwards, starting from lying in bed and proceeding as if viewing a movie in your video on rewind.

So, you're in bed and the lights are off. Then you are turning the light off. Then the light is on and you are deciding that it's time to turn it off. Then you are just getting into bed. And so on, all the way back to the moment that you woke up in the morning.

This exercise is not easy so don't worry if you get distracted and forget the sequence. However if you do, and you will, you must start again from the beginning. After a while most people fall asleep,

ABOVE Reviewing the day in reverse is much less disturbing to the body than sleeping pills.

LEFT AND PREVIOUS PAGE Even the most routine activities become rituals when done with total attention.

and because their minds have been focused, yet relaxed and unwinding, they have a deep and restful sleep.

In time, with practice you will be able to go over more and more of your day. Quite automatically you will begin to notice recurring patterns, but because of the backwards sequence you will find yourself less critical and judgmental of yourself. Because you are not giving yourself a hard time about how you should have acted, what you should have said, etc., you will notice that the next day you will be more alert and naturally able to respond to situations authentically and more appropriately. This will take some repeated practice of the exercise, so stay with it and experiment. You may be pleasantly surprised at the changes that take place in your life.

FOLLOW YOUR RAINBOW

As real and natural as any physical thirst, we possess a longing of the heart. Anatomical dissection will never reveal its location and no machine can measure its true pulse. Its voice runs through music and poetry; its light shines out of great art; it lives in the laughter of children and in the touch of lovers.

But to give it words, limits it. In almost all religious texts, in myths and allegories, there is a garden of Eden, a place of primeval purity, of total freedom, beauty, and of boundless love. It is the place where we all feel we have once lived, and however our lives unfold, it is there we are striving to return.

Occasionally we receive glimpses of it. Sometimes at magical moments in our lives, we even feel that it might be right here on earth. Don't discount such feelings. Don't dismiss the indefinable inner longing as just another idle daydream. We all have a yearning for something higher and greater than ourselves, but all too often in the rush of day-to-day details we neglect our thirst and hunger and get bogged down in the chaos around us.

A child's unceasing wonder in the face of creation must be what is meant when it is said that "Unless you become like little children, you cannot enter the kingdom of heaven." To a child, wonder comes naturally; to us it is a longing. It poises, always on the edge of our being, as a mystery to be experienced one day – but never now.

Trust your longing. Give it room to expand and grow. If you nourish it, for sure it will nourish you!

PART IV
AT YOUR LEISURE

RELATING

IT TAKES TWO TO TANGO

"I get high with a little help from my friends."
The Beatles

The growth and evolution of this book is a work of love. We sit at our desk working and reworking the exercises and the text, arranging and re-arranging, adding and deleting, all in an effort to produce the best work possible. To be simple, clear, and precise brings satisfaction to our efforts. Yet, in order for the circle of creativity to be completed, one more element is sorely needed – you the reader. Without you there is no joy, no true fulfillment.

We want to share, and we need to share and connect with our fellow man. It is so much more fun to travel the road of self-discovery in the company of friends. We inspire, excite, and support one another. By the sharing of ourselves, we are in no way diminished. Rather we can expand and grow easier and faster.

If you have been experimenting with the exercises, you will be feeling an opening and an expansion in the range and quality of choices available to you in life.

And in this way a very natural urge arises to share what you are learning with others and to experiment together with them.

This section presents a number of exercises to be done with other people. Some are quite intimate, to be shared with a close loved-one, while others can be done at the office, supermarket or anywhere.

Remember what we discussed in the first secret about starting from where you are? You may be well into the swing of things by now, but your partner may be new to these exercises. Start at a point from where they are ready to launch off, start easily, and let the interest and the confidence build up in your partner before tackling exercises that may be more challenging. And, as always, have a good time with it!

The exercises in this section are all different types of relating techniques, to be done with another person. It could be a husband or wife, a lover or friend, a parent or child, or perhaps someone you would like to get to know better.

All of us on this planet are interrelated with each other and our environment. A seed cannot sprout without earth and water. The tree that grows from this seed needs its roots to sink deep into the earth. And when it grows tall it gives its leaves and fruits and flowers back to the earth to nourish it. When we dance with our environment and with each other in this way, we move through life beautifully.

This section provides us with techniques of relating in new and more alive ways, of letting a fresh breeze blow through the patterns of all our relationships, letting us see with new eyes and dance to the music that always plays deep down in our hearts.

■ LOVING WITHOUT TECHNIQUE

The most basic instinct within man is for survival:

self preservation. Following just behind is the instinct for survival of the species. This instinct is fueled by a very normal function, which even the birds and the bees have no problem with – sex.

Yet, among us humans it has become one of the most widely misunderstood activities of all. At times repressed and hidden, while at other times flaunted and raised to glorious heights, it rarely is in its normal and natural position as simply one of man's natural functions.

In an ideal modern society sexual activity plays several roles. First, to continue the species, in numbers that are appropriate for the maximum benefit for all. Second, as a form of pleasure, recreation and enjoyment for the individual. Third, as a form of intimacy, sharing and joy between two people. And fourth, as a basic energy of life which in time is transformed into more subtle energies as man grows and matures.

In most cultures on the planet today none of these functions are being fulfilled. In a sexually repressed country like India far too many children are born to be comfortably supported. Because of prevalent attitudes, sex is not enjoyed, providing minimal pleasure for the male and even less for the female – what to say of intimacy? In India religion controls sex.

In a sexually freer society such as America where the concept of birth control is accepted, the population growth is more reasonable. Sex is more out in the open and enjoyed. Yet it has become a tool for business – selling everything from cars to mouthwash, as well as a weapon of power in the battle of the sexes. Even politicians use it to slander their opponents. In America big business and the power mongers control sex.

In a place like Holland which is probably the most liberal country in the world today, sex has come so much out in the open, has been so demystified and has entered into the classroom where its mystery and possibility of deep intimacy is being stripped away. In Holland educators control sex.

What has gone wrong in the world to bring sex into such a sorry state? Why has religion poked its nose into sex making it dirty? In German genitals are called *die Schamteile* – the parts of shame. Why has man tried to control woman's sexuality over the ages? Why have politics and business gotten so involved in it?

Simply because sex is such a basic and instinctive energy it becomes a powerful tool in the hands of those who seek power and control over others. In every society there exists a taboo against either sex or death – the beginning and the end of the life cycle. The two flip sides of the same coin. In a more sane and civilized world sex and death would be accepted and celebrated as natural phenomenas that happen to all of us. As it is, we fear one or the other and this fear is used by the power hungry to achieve control over others.

Ironically, a new development has recently occurred in the world which is forcing us to re-examine our attitudes and relationship to both sex and death. This development has connected sex and death in a startling way. This phenomena is a disease called AIDS.

It is a further reflection upon the sad state of our world when such a lethal and ugly occurrence is needed before we sit up and take notice and try to reassess our sexuality and the role of sex in our lives. Still, if we are able to rise to the challenge and make the best of this situation, there is the opportunity of bringing in a new age of sexual conduct which is more sane than the extremes we are presently dealing with in different parts of the world.

We believe that AIDS is a lesson for us all. Our immune system is normally a friendly army that guards our physical bodies. Somehow we have become increasingly careless and negative in regards to ourselves. The very gift of life is being undermined. Examine the rising crime rate, threats to the ecology, nuclear build-ups and a host of other serious problems that we are facing today. At the root of it all appears a universally accepted grand

PREVIOUS PAGE Playfulness transforms lust into intimacy.

ABOVE Different cultures have had different ideas about transforming sexual energy.

RIGHT Lying cozy and quiet a circle of energy forms between the male and female polarities.

concept of the ego, which states that man is master of the universe. We run around conquering. Conquering each other, our rivers, forests and animals. Now we are even challenging outer space. What ever happened to co-existence?

On good days we strut around feeling that we are the greatest thing on earth – the rulers of all. On bad days we get hit with the flip side of this coin. We feel a deep unworthiness. We are no good and only deserve all the punishments existence delivers us, (well supported by the idea of original sin).

Neither of these concepts approaches the truth. We are part of life, and because we are, arguably, the most conscious form of life we can affect our planet the most – for good or bad. The choice is ours.

In sex the choice is also ours, for there, too, desire to rule and feelings of unworthiness and inadequacy can easily enter if we fall into old habits. The following are not sex techniques, exercises or methods to practice. Enough sex manuals are already on the market. But the real reason why we shy away from any techniques is because they can be yet another tool for controlling the behavior of the individual. All do's and don'ts, even with the best intentions behind them, cramp our style, limit our individuality, and take away our power and response-ability.

The first point to consider is to please yourself. Begin by pleasing yourself and you will be happy, and in turn will want to please the other, effortlessly. Then pleasing is just an overflow of affection. If you aim at pleasing the other first you fall out of touch with yourself. Then a game of sexual politics ensues and eventually resentment is bound to arise because you're not getting what you want. You may blame the other, but really it's your fault for starting off on the wrong foot. Please yourself and you can work any problems out. Really, pleasing yourself is the least selfish way to be.

Pleasing yourself depends on discovering how your energy wants to move. Sometimes there is great excitement, mounting tension, and dramatic release. At other times the energy is more like a deep cool river. Sometimes the energy changes from one moment to another, as the river hits some rapids or a waterfall. Sometimes wild, sometimes soft, sometimes sexy at other times more sensual: whatever the energy, try to get in touch with it and flow with the river rather than trying to fight your way upstream or impose your shoulds and should nots.

Discovering how your energy wants to go in turn relies on your being present in the moment, both to yourself and to your partner, rather than going through a stock routine of moves – stroke there, push here, nibble this, breathe heavy. This kind of performance becomes boring very quickly and people have to change partners to maintain interest. Then sex becomes nothing more than just letting off steam.

Being in the moment is easiest when we connect, atune and harmonize with ourself and with our partner. Then sex is music. Not the noise of instruments playing helter skelter, but sweet celestial music.

Much of sexual connecting happens on a non-verbal level. Communicate, connect and stimulate the whole body, yours and your partner's, not just the sexual organs. Introduce massage, oils, music, personal cleanliness, and a nice environment to your lovemaking.

There is also room for verbal communication, before, during and after, expressing our pleasures and desires to the other. We all have personal preferences as to what turns us on. Your partner may be preparing an incredible steak dinner for you and will be hurt if you wait until it is ready to tell him that you are a vegetarian.

The threat of AIDS has brought a whole new dimension into sexual activity. Some of the competitiveness, performance anxiety and general pressure around sex has lessened. Cuddling is becoming more popular and its potential for intimacy is being explored. People are relating more genuinely and viewing each other less as sexual objects.

The use of condoms is cultivating a whole new level of humor. It is sometimes difficult to maintain an attitude of serious lust while fumbling to extricate a condom from its wrapper – the lighter side of sex.

Monogamy is back in fashion. Platonic relationships do have a place in our lives. More friendliness and sharing between men and women becomes possible. Even celibacy is a viable alternative. Careful sexual activity may lower the quantity of one's sexual partners but quality may actually rise. Also on the rise is touching and other forms of friendly physical contact – careful but physical.

Earlier we mentioned the two great taboos, sex and death. In India sex is kept hidden. Most Indian women are never naked, not even in front of their husbands. Even kissing is not allowed to be shown in Indian movies. Meanwhile, death is no big deal. People are dying out in the open. In the city of Benares the streets are packed with devout Hindus who have come to die in this holy place.

In the west people don't discuss death, they don't even die, they just pass away. We westerners feel very uncomfortable looking death in the face.

It is just possible that we are heading into a new age where we are able to get beyond the death taboo and bring fresh understanding and dignity into a process that, like it or not, happens to all of us. Already hospices are springing up that cater to the dying and their families and a new consciousness about death is growing. As we begin to assume greater responsibility for our sexuality, for the way we live, and for the way we die we are living more in balance with ourselves and with existence. Through this balance we can affect the whole world and bring more sanity, clarity, joy and love to a planet that at this time is sorely in need of all of our help.

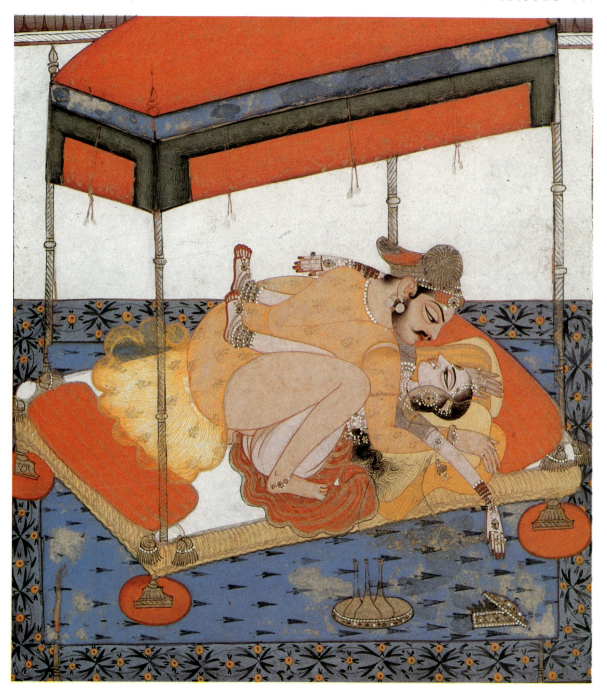

BEING THERE

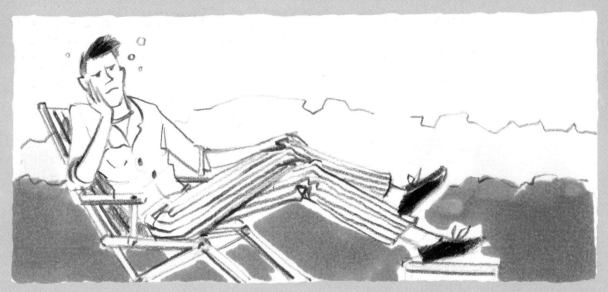

In order to understand assertiveness we need first to describe the nonassertive personality. Nonassertive people bottle up their energy. They hold back, putting other people ahead of themselves, and end up coming last. To be kind and considerate to others is certainly a virtue if balanced by other qualities, but the nonassertive person, by placing himself last, ends up with a low level of self-esteem and a lack of confidence. Often they are sensitive and aware people, but they do not let this side show. In their desire to be liked they take the back seat to such a degree that others take advantage of them and push them around. They do not allow their energy to flow or to move. They fear making mistakes and as a result do not live up to their capacity. They lead shallow and unfulfilled lives.

One of the reasons nonassertive people are the way they are is because they do not want to be aggressive. It seems that being aggressive is the negative side of the assertiveness coin. Aggressive people always put themselves first. They may be very out front in doing this, or possibly do it in a more roundabout way, sneakily getting back at others who get in their way. Aggressive people have a false sense of self-worth. Theirs is not a true self-esteem. They act tough and push their way to the top, fearing deep down all the while that they are not good enough.

Both of these stances are attempts on the part of the person to hide their true self. And this is the great pity. For everyone is a unique and beautiful person in his own right. The assertive person is aware of this. They do not put themselves before or after others, but consider themselves equal to others. They take responsibility for themselves by expressing their wants, needs, thoughts and feelings. They speak for themselves and show their sensitivity by being able to listen to others as well. They have learned to be honest with others by being honest with themselves. They allow their energy to flow and therefore are creative. For creativity is not restricted to a talented few. Anyone can be creative if they will only allow themselves to be so.

Non assertive people are afraid of hurting other people and of doing the wrong thing. Aggressive people are used to being hurt, and hide it by hurting first. It is their protection. Assertive people are honest first and foremost, and this, balanced by their respect for themselves and others, allows them to take risks, to be themselves and yet to be liked and enjoyed by others.

The exercise that follows this Secret is one in being assertive. This quality is one that we all possess, and yet too few people in our society have developed it sufficiently. We rely too much on a convention based on being polite and hiding our true feelings. This we develop to such a degree that there comes a point at which we lose touch with our true feelings, so hidden are they under layers and layers of convention.

Many people will hesitate to try the exercise, not so much for fear of expressing their true selves, but because they fear that there may be only a hollow shell underneath, devoid of true feeling. Yet others fear that there is so much boiling under the surface that if they give it a chance to come out it will be an unstoppable volcano.

These two attitudes often emerge during the course of deep body-work sessions. It has been the experience of all deep body-workers, especially Rebalancers, that as places in the body holding onto deep trauma (early emotion or conflict of any kind) are touched, people become afraid. In this fear they feel as if they would rather stay as they are living, with the familiar, even though it may be very painful and restrictive, rather than face up to what may happen. The anticipation of what could

happen is that frightening. When people break through and face whatever it is they fear, they invariably cannot believe that they were so afraid in the first place.

Some people have described getting in touch with their real nature as being like a traffic jam during an accident. The traumas or fears that caused us to shut down in the first place have caused things to get bottled up. When the block starts to clear, it is they that are the first cars to get moving. Not only that, but until normal traffic is restored the other cars jammed up for long periods of time are also anxious to start moving again. Many cars are coming almost at once – fear, anger, tears mixed with laughter, joy, pain and sorrow. It is all so intense and confusing, it is hard to

know what is going on and why it is all happening at once. It doesn't continue this way. If we allow the flow to come naturally and to take its due course, very quickly traffic is moving at a regular rhythm again. Only if we fight and try to control the rhythm does the flow get disturbed and hampered.

Be kind and gentle with yourself; assertiveness

is natural and normal behavior. Although many of us are out of touch with our natural selves, being out of touch does not mean that the natural is not there. It is always there and available; we need only to relax and tap into it. For some it is easier than for others. Do not compare yourself – there is no need. Start slowly at your own rhythm and let the pace change as it will. Whenever you feel you can, take more small risks in exposing yourself. As you do so you will get positive feedback from yourself and others. This will encourage you to bring it into your day-to-day life more and more.

It is worthwhile remembering that there may be some people who think they have an investment in keeping you the way you are. Pick someone to do relating exercises with who will not be too threatened by seeing different sides of yourself. If you truly feel there are no such people in your life at the moment, you may want to consider doing a

human potential group of some sort or another. In controlled group situations where people come together specifically to grow and explore themselves, it is easily possible to share oneself with people who were, before the group, total strangers. Because the very structure is designed to be a safe situation for opening to oneself it is sometimes initially easier to explore different possibilities than in so-called real life. The conventions and rules of the group are different than they may be in your home situation, where years of habit and acting in a certain way and being known in a certain way tend to hold you into a mold that you are trying to break out of.

Once the energy is moving, once the traffic jam is dissolved, it is then easier to transform your day-to-day life by returning more and more to your true nature, to the state that the mystics refer to as your original face.

■ MUTUAL ATTENTION

It's time to go for a walk. The length of this exercise is measured in steps rather than minutes. The structure is simple.

You and your partner go for a stroll, preferably in a quiet place free from distractions. On the outward leg of the journey one person talks while the other person simply listens without comment. On the way back the other person gets their chance. The objective is to express your needs and wants to the other without any expectation of fulfillment. You are not making demands on the other, not being aggressive or laying a trip on anyone. You are simply being honest and sincere in communicating with someone close to you. You are unburdening yourself of all the big and small things that you feel you need and want from this person, and also in life in general.

Because there is no pressure on the other to fulfill your needs, you can be quite outrageous, revealing secret desires that you would normally never talk about for fear of rejection or because they seem impossible to attain. It is a chance to really expose yourself and through this sharing to grow closer together. Just as best friends at high school open their hearts to each other to share their hopes, fears and desires, and through this form strong bonds of friendship, you share.

Even people who have very open lines of communication in their relationship are astounded by the new information exchanged in exercises like this. And it also often happens that people find ways of meeting each other's wants and needs in new and unexpected ways. Because we are not actually expecting them to be met, when it happens it is an incredible experience.

Even if nothing concrete comes out of the sharing, people find great benefit derived from it. Just to communicate frankly, but without any pressure, is reward in itself. It allows us to be assertive with those around and close to us without hurting them. We feel good afterwards, and so too does the other person.

1 When listening, just listen with all your attention and no judgments.

2 When talking be courageous, say what's really on your mind.

We went to a movie the other day to discover that, due to an error in the newspaper, the movie we had gone to see was not playing. Other people had also come to the movie and it was interesting to observe the different types of reaction. Some people just accepted what had happened and quietly left. Others were angry and aggressive towards the theater manager, which made the manager angry and defensive in turn. Eventually the angry ones left as well, storming out amid great huffing and puffing. At this point one lady approached the manager and spoke to him in a relaxed and friendly way, explaining that she understood there was nothing the manager could do about the situation but he should also understand that she and the rest of us had chosen his theater over others and had made a trip in vain. Immediately the manager, no longer having to be on the defensive, could think clearly again and came up with an idea. All of us that were still there received two complimentary tickets to the movies. Now we felt better, as did the poor manager. We left with a smile instead of a frown. This beautifully illustrates the power of assertiveness.

In your daily life you will be given many chances to practice assertiveness: at the supermarket, in the bank, at work and at play. If you can manage to do so without putting the emphasis on the results but rather on the actual activity of standing up and being yourself, your general self-esteem will be bolstered immensely. Life will become less of a struggle and more of an amusing and entertaining play.

■ TRUST WALK

This is an exercise in caring and trusting which stimulates a heightened sense of intimacy between two people.

The only tools necessary are: a nice place to take a stroll and a scarf or anything else that can be used as a blindfold. The blindfold is placed on one person who then has to rely on the other to be led around safely. The other, the eyes, then leads the blind one on a walk, taking every care to help him to relax more and more. Warning of any rocks or steps, or of any pitfalls should be given nonverbally and guidance is so precise it becomes a dance. As much as possible, give the blind person nice sensual experiences – brushing a soft leaf or grasses on his face or body, playing with water, walking barefoot on soft earth or moss, moving between shadows and light that penetrate the blindfold. And there are many more possibilities to bring the senses more life and vibrancy. After a while the roles can be reversed.

To trust in another's guidance completely, as well as to care for another's well-being in every moment, are wonderful ways of sharing ourselves with another. Usually these qualities are highly esteemed, yet we mostly learn to be wary of each other, and to trust no one completely because they

With each step, an ever growing bond of trust develops.

1 Gently guide your "blind" partner.

2 The squeeze on the neck is the signal to open the eyes.

3 The "snap shot" will be a delightful surprise.

could hurt us. Even caring for others often does not come naturally. It's not that we don't feel caring, but all too often we just have not had opportunities to practice the ways and means to show our appreciation.

Even when done among strangers this exercise creates an immediate closeness. It is quite remarkable to witness a strong bond of friendship between two people develop so quickly. It can take an already established relationship into an even deeper intimacy.

■ SNAP SHOTS

This is an extension of the blindfold exercise which brings in the added dimension of a heightened perceptive state. Having become familiar and relaxed with walking around without use of his eyes, the blind person does without the blindfold this time, but keeps his eyes shut. The leader rests his hand on the back of the blind one's neck. Whenever the hand gently squeezes at the top of the neck for a moment, the blind one opens his eyes for the same length of time. One image is caught in the mind's eye in the same way that a camera freezes one instant in time,.

The leader's job is to compose the picture, bringing in their creativity, humor and insight – seeing the world through two sets of eyes brings it into a stronger focus. Meanwhile the blind one is relaxing in the darkness until suddenly there is an image, clear and strong, flashed at him with no expectation as to what it might be – a delightful, funny, fleeting, and haunting surprise. Whatever it is, it is of this moment, frozen in time and space. And often the technique creates such a strong image that you will remember it for years to come.

■ SILENT COMMUNION

This is a simple and beautiful way of connecting with a lover, whether you have been together three days or thirty years.

1 As you sit together with closed eyes feel the energy focusing in the area of the heart.

2 Gently open your eyes, keeping the gaze soft and receptive.

Choose a nice piece of instrumental music, thirty to fourty-five minutes long, to play during this exercise.

Sit comfortably on the floor or in chairs, facing one another with knees touching. Get used to this contact for a couple of minutes, letting yourselves settle into a manner of meeting that you may not be used to.

Hold hands, close your eyes, and tune in to the energy passing between you. It may be a strong current, like electricity, or it could be a subtle wave moving gently. Whatever you feel, even if it is very little, is fine.

Once you are familiar with whatever is transpiring, begin to focus the attention on your chest. With each breath let the chest relax a little more, and as relaxation deepens, you will find a tuning of the two energies taking place effortlessly much like a baby at its mother's breast relaxes into her warmth and support. You will notice your breath becoming deeper and easier, and can hear the breath of your partner doing the same.

Gradually, two individuals, now coming closer to being one energy, begin to focus on an area in the center of the chest – the heart. As the breath rises and falls in smooth waves, the heart is felt to awaken its radiant stirring, spreading outwards to envelop the two of you in a single field of love.

Anywhere from fifteen to twenty-five minutes into the exercise, you open your eyes. There is a soft effortless way of looking out of the eyes. It is not a staring, an attempt to penetrate and over-power with one's gaze. Rather imagine that your eyes are not at the front of your head but in the center, a couple of inches behind your physical eyes. In this way the gaze is receptive, inviting and very easy to maintain. The feeling is that you could sit this way comfortably for ever. It is so soft and natural, as if the very doorways of the soul were open and totally accessible to each other.

The end of the music signals the conclusion of the exercise. Looking becomes hugging and what you do next is totally up to you in the moment.

1 Miming is a great form of expression, everything can be conveyed through your movements.

2 Heart to heart.

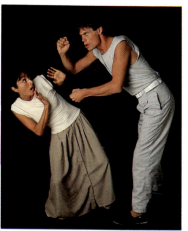

3 Anger, rage, fear, the possibilities are endless.

Whatever happens, when you separate physically, you will be carrying around a little more of your friend in your heart than ever before.

■ NO TALKING

To bring freshness and a new sense of creativity into any relationship try, for one or two hours a day for a week, to communicate without using any words. The rules are simple: no talking, yet being together exchanging information and feelings – communicating what you would normally say in words, using body language instead. This does not mean just being in the same room and doing separate activities – this is a real meeting. Making love, massaging, eating, and dancing are all obvious ways. Fine as an introduction, to get into the swing of things, and as a warm-up for more unusual activities.

Miming, acting out what you wish to communicate, is a challenge. Singing together, painting pictures to convey messages, works well. Or imagine that you are two babies who have not yet learned to speak and are playing together. Or, perhaps you are monkeys, munching bananas and scratching each others' backs. Even the simplest activities, like washing the car, take on a whole new level when done nonverbally.

After a few days you will at times be spontaneously creating ingenious and often hilarious forms of relating.

This exercise can also be done by more than two people. And, after having tried the previous nonverbal connecting exercise, it can throw you back effortlessly into feeling your heart. Perhaps you will want to try this exercise for a few days before experimenting with the other. It's up to you, but certainly you will notice that very quickly this exercise seems to take on a life of its own. Furthermore, as you feel more and more comfortable with it, you find yourself communicating more often to people in a new way for the rest of your day.

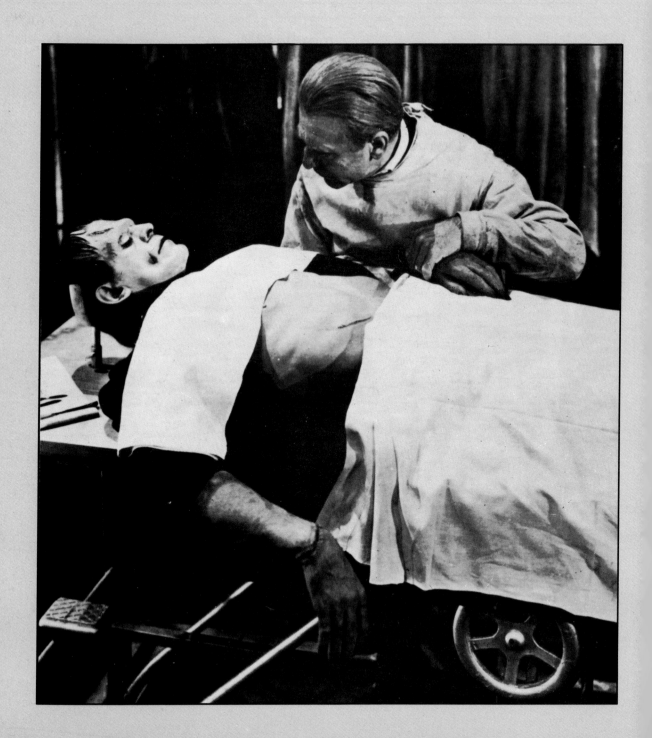

THE IN CROWD

The marathon runner punishes his body by pushing it. The starved intellectual disowns his by giving it no importance. The alcoholic abuses his body with what he puts into it. The overworked housewife neglects hers. The prostitute demeans her body by treating it as an object and the executive ignores his, because he hasn't got time to give it the attention it deserves.

These are generalities, not necessarily, but all too often, true. The mystics maintain that the body is a temple and is to be treated with reverence and love. So why is it that we misuse our bodies so much?

One of the main reasons is that man, especially western man, until quite recently has made a separation between all the parts of himself that make up his whole totality.

To live in balance is to recognize that body, mind and heart are all interconnected parts of a greater whole. That whole is us. The mind that gives the command to the hand that reaches out to feel and express our love to another, is all one and the same. Holistic medicine is one example of a trend in the west which examines and treats the whole person rather than just the part that is showing a symptom.

How can there be any separation? Can we leave our body on the subway or forget our mind at work? It is obvious that we are not just a set of parts randomly put together, but a whole, working in one harmony. Couldn't this unseen and untouchable thing be what we call the soul, or the spirit, or our true nature – the very unity of our parts? What, after all, made the Frankenstein monster unacceptable to human beings except that he was just a collection of different body pieces sewn together?

If we ignore either the body, the mind, or the heart, we become like a Frankenstein artifact – a bunch of disconnected pieces held together by surgical thread. Without the soul we lack the true thread which binds us together and makes us one.

Honor all the different parts that come together to create the unique creature that is you, and your life will be enhanced a million-fold. For you will then come into contact with that very nebulous thing called soul. You will know it and live it. You will experience your own true nature.

■ MAGNIFY YOUR MADNESS

Anything we hold onto gets held. Anything we let go of, goes. This is a simple law of life. Seasons come and go, and to everything there is a season: another law of existence. Man in his folly tries to outwit the laws of life: yet another of life's laws.

Put these three laws into action and in certain situations what you get is a form of behavior called neurosis. We all have forms of behavior that could be termed neurotic. A baby who sucks his thumb is normal. The same person as an adult sucking his thumb is considered neurotic – at the very least. In its season thumb-sucking was appropriate. In a later season it is a sign of someone trying to hold onto a form of behavior that is no longer appropriate.

Thumb-sucking in itself is no big deal. Others may be shocked, they may ridicule you, or in the more broad-minded societies they may just chuckle at your expense and let you do your thing. The problem lies elsewhere, at the heart of the neuroses itself. For the very act of holding onto an old pattern takes a lot of effort. This effort must be made and re-made all the time, in every moment. And even though the effort is made unconsciously, like breathing, it still takes a great deal of energy. As a result we have less and less energy for other activities. Neuroses take up most of our time and strength. Therefore the very activities that comprise neurotic behavior throw us out of balance.

There are some people who are able to transform their neuroses, to channel it into productive activity. These people are not usually even referred to as neurotic. They are called great artists, business tycoons, performers, and even presidents. They are called eccentric rather than neurotic and their countries are proud of them.

There is an even rarer being who has been able to use their neuroses in such a positive manner that they have fallen into a totally new kind of balance. They have created within themselves a new law of existence. One that is able to embrace all the other laws, permitting them all to function at the same time without getting caught up by any single one. In this way they have risen above the normal laws. In their world, even if there is neurosis, it is just another energy. It does not produce conflict within the individual. He or she is at peace with him or herself and with the world. These blessed people are called the mystics. The creative neurotics, the eccentrics, take their particular forms of neuroses and in some way transform them into a creative form. Woody Allen is a popular example of someone who, in acting out his neuroses for everyone to see, transforms them into humor, compassion, love, not to mention fame and riches. Mozart was said to be quite a strange fellow. And what about Van Gogh, or Howard Hughes? Sometimes the scales tip in the other direction and we get a Napoleon or a Hitler.

Society has a strange relationship with its bad apples. It tries to suppress the neurotic at every step until the neurotic gets so powerful that whole countries turn and support their neurotic in all kinds of crazy ventures. In the very act of suppression, society supports the worst aspects of neurotic behavior, and gives it a power way beyond anyone's ability to handle. In trying to contain the energy of neuroses, society creates a certain kind of friction, which eventually leads to an explosion of nuclear proportions.

The mystic uses a totally different approach. He or she does not fight neuroses. He embraces it close to his heart and then lets it go. He accepts neurosis as part of his life in that moment, and also acknowledges that change is always happening. The world is turning, and the seasons are changing.

There is a Zen saying, "Sitting silently, doing nothing, spring comes, and the grass grows by itself." This is the basis of the mystic's understanding. He acknowledges and enjoys each and every moment so fully and totally that he is able to let it go. For he knows there is nothing to be gained from holding on, and he trusts that the next moment will also bring something fresh and fulfilling.

He sees there is no reason to struggle and to fight, or to push a river when it is already flowing. And living every moment totally, he is able to let the moment go and with empty hands to totally greet the next moment and all that it holds.

When the Zen people speak of sitting silently and doing nothing they are often misunderstood. The statues that we see today of Gautam the Buddha, the Indian mystic, show only one aspect of his life. They show a man sitting perfectly still and composed in silent meditation. In fact, Buddha traveled nonstop for forty years spreading his message across thousands of miles. As a result, it is still alive today, 2,500 years later. Rather than representing an ideal in itself, the statues symbolize his inner state. A state of such inner relaxation and peace that nothing could throw him out of balance. Much of the behavior that led Buddha to his balance may easily be termed neurotic. He was a prince who gave up his kingdom to pursue a life of extreme hardship and deprivation in order to follow a dream. He wanted to know himself, and the quest eventually became the goal. Neurosis was transformed.

We too can do the same. Perhaps you have no aspirations to be a mystic at this time in your life. Still, by following the path the mystics talk about we can live a much richer and more creative way. We can at least stop being drained and tortured by our neuroses and start enjoying and learning from them. For neurosis does have a strong power of its own. It is up to us to choose wisely and to use this power in positive ways.

What we have here is a two-point plan. First, we acknowledge our neurosis. We say hello to it, and how are you today? We embrace it because it is a part of us, and, if we oppose it, we oppose ourselves and cause ourselves pain. We embrace it, as much as we can, and then we let it go. That is the second part of the exercise. Neither do we fight nor do we cling to neurosis.

Why would anyone be silly enough to hold onto neurosis? Because it is familiar, we are used to it, and it is truly part of us. We may be fighting and resisting it, but, without it, what would we have to keep us busy and occupied, and how would we know who we are? Neurosis is like a bad late-night movie that we are too tired to turn off. It holds us hypnotized in its boring spell. Break loose from the spell, and suddenly you are left with life, rich and full – and right now!

In truth, the only way to really understand is through experiencing for yourself a new way of using your neurotic energies. Begin with this simple exercise and learn to contact your neuroses, embrace them and let them go.

You can begin alone in your room. Start by pacing around, twitching, wringing your hands, or any other neurotic signals that you enjoy or have seen others doing.

By acting out neuroses in a self-loving, self-accepting way, you are not increasing the neurotic pattern, but rather letting it run its course, which in due time will finish it.

Look into a mirror and make funny faces. Growl, scowl, fume, look helpless, aggressive, weak, or overpowering. Be sad, morose, sexy or stupid. Change the faces of your neuroses into as many different ways as you can think of. No need to limit yourself in any way.

Once you have practiced alone, it is time to try with another person. Ask someone close to you, with whom you feel comfortable, if you can act out in a neurotic way with him. All he has to do is to be there for you as an audience.

If the other is also a bit courageous he can also join in acting out his neurotic habits. Now there are two neurotics relating to each other. It is not the easiest of techniques, as you are attempting to overcome your embarrassment and reveal to another a part of yourself that you usually try to keep hidden. Take courage from the fact that when we try to hide our neuroses we rarely succeed anyway. Plus, in hiding them, we succeed in merely pushing these actions deeper into our physical and psychological make-up. By trying to

CAT'S CRADLE
1 A carpet or a cushion to sit on makes it more comfortable.

2 Hold this position for a couple of breaths.

3 For even more stretch and balancing, rock back and forth.

hide our neuroses we are actually nurturing neurotic behavior and increasing its impact upon ourselves. By sharing it with someone we actually let go of our patterns. Furthermore, by consciously choosing to reveal them, they change from deep, dark and ominous secrets that we are fighting to hide, into amusing idiosyncrasies that we can actually laugh about. Neuroses lose their seriousness, their charge, and their ability to make us miserable.

Try the exercise; have fun with it; be prepared to shed some light on the dark recesses of your being. Your inner monsters live in darkness. In the light they turn out not to be monsters at all but merely imaginary shadows.

■ DOUBLE STRETCHES
Following is a series of exercises to be done with a partner. They are intended to be fun and another opportunity to explore your ways of relating to another person. Do them in a light hearted spirit

and you will both reap the benefits of learning to stretch your bodies in new ways.

■ CAT'S CRADLE
Sit with your knees up facing your partner and hands hooked into each other's, with toes touching.

Raise one leg up together with your partner's keeping your feet sole-to-sole and your legs as straight as possible. Then bring the second leg up, leaning back and maintaining your balance, keeping your arms extended.

■ DRAGON BUTTERFLY
Stand side by side with the outsides of the inside feet touching. Reach over with your outside arms and grip hands in the front. Turn your heads and meet eyes, and slowly stretch over to the side away from each other raising your inner arm as you do so, until it is completely extended as far over away from each other as you can, twisting with your

DRAGON BUTTERFLY

1 Make eye contact and start to bend.

2 For best stretch keep shoulders and arms parallel to the ceiling. Don't forget to breathe!

3 Take it easy and feel your connection.

FORWARD AND BACK

1 Note that her legs are well supported and their hands interlocked.

2 Her pelvis drops forward creating a smooth arc.

3 In this picture the male model is leaning forward a little too much. Keep the back straight, head more back.

OVER THE TOP

I Hold this position until you feel that contact has been made and both partners are relaxed.

2 Move slowly. Trust your partner.

3 Stay in touch with your partner's stretch by asking for feedback.

shoulder backwards to prevent you from leaning too far forward.

Now bend your knees and drop a little farther over and then straighten your legs again: this increases the stretch a little. Breathe deeply into the extended parts of your sides.

Come up by bending you knees first and curling into each other. Close your eyes and just relax together in that position. Now change sides and do it again, stretching the other side of your body.

■ FORWARD AND BACKWARD

This exercise is easier than it looks. The supported person stands with her feet together and back to the her partner, holding at the wrists, bracing the backs of her heels with the outside of her partner's foot. She slowly falls forward leading with the pelvis. It is important to lead with the pelvis even though at first this might feel a little scary. As she falls forward the supporter leans back slightly. The supported person breathes deeply into her chest raising her head backwards. Now the one supporting her gently pulls her back into the standing position.

Now the supported one flexes over forward with her head going towards her knees. Keeping her legs straight, if possible, she lets her weight pull her forward slightly onto her toes. And then she bends her knees and rolls up through her knees, and her pelvis and slowly up through her back to the top of her head, taking each part of her body gently step by step.

Now switch roles.

■ OVER THE TOP

Sitting back to back one partner brings her knees up, keeping her feet flat on the ground, and leans backwards slowly over the back of her partner. If the person underneath who is being stretched forward finds his legs are too stiff to stay straight, start by putting a pillow under the knees, allowing the legs to bend a little.

The person on top extends her arms back,

which increases the stretch of the one underneath, and both breath deeply. Remember to give each other continual feedback about how you are doing.

The one on top gently slides down until she is sitting again while at the same time the other raises himself. They then sit back-to-back with closed eyes. Now reverse it.

■ RAVE ON!

We have all at some time or another been at a loss to reply to questions such as, "How are you?" or "What's new and interesting?" It is a strange feeling to be asked this question when nothing pops into our heads as a reply. Certainly it is not because nothing is happening, but rather we are out of touch in that moment with ourselves. It may even feel like there is nothing going on with us at that moment, but it's only because we have lost touch with all the varied processes that are taking place within us at any one given time.

By getting in touch with our inner workings and by being able to communicate them to others we add a new wealth to our relationships.

These are two simple exercises in getting in touch and communicating ourselves to ourselves and to others.

The first one you do alone.

Simply sit down for an hour and write down anything that you are thinking or feeling. If you cannot sit still that long, carry around a pad and, while puttering around the house or going for a walk, keep jotting down anything that comes into your head. "But nothing is coming." Good, just jot that down. "This is silly, I know it is all going to be very boring (keep writing). My nose is itchy, and I need to pee, and... and..."

Just let it come, uninhibited and uncensored. The more you let just anything come up and be recorded, the more interesting become the things you write. Not all the time: it does go in waves, but the creative faculty and the listening faculty both

1 Talk to yourself without inhibition.

2 Tell your partner everything that's on your mind.

engage and rise to the challenge. Try it and see.

After writing for a while you may want to try a dictaphone or tape recorder. More difficult at first because you are also listening to yourself speak and that can make you self-conscious. But in time this too becomes easy.

The second exercise involves a partner. For five minutes just report to your partner everything that you are experiencing. Then switch over. Then switch back and do another round. You will be amazed at how much we do feel and think at all times that we are barely aware of. We all do constantly carry on an inner dialogue with ourselves, and the more conscious it becomes the more we are masters of our destinies.

■ REVIEWING CONTRACTS

In nearly every form of relating there are certain contracts built in: the laws of a country, the rules of any sport, moral codes, dress codes, and codes we all agree to conform to. These are contracts developed over time, and formally set down and recognized. There are also less formal contracts found everywhere in our lives. Even with our pets we have contracts: I will feed you and play with you, you will guard my property and wag your tail when you see me.

In reviewing contracts we seek to bring into the open, into clear language, the small unwritten contracts that have evolved over time in relationships with those closest to us. With our partners, with lovers and friends and with our children, we have these little arrangements: if I take out the garbage at night, you will make the morning tea. If you're going to be late coming home, you will call and let me know. If I tell you my secret, you must not tell anyone else.

These are simple, usually unspoken contracts that nevertheless mean a lot to us all, and their neglect and misuse can lead to resentment and heartache. On the other hand, by reviewing and renegotiating them we stand to gain insight into each other's idiosyncratic ways of doing things ("Oh, now I understand why you always do it that way!"), understanding of each other's difficulties ("Wow, there's more to this than I'd ever have thought!"), clearing the way for less misunderstanding in communicating ("But I thought you thought that I meant you should do this when actually you must have thought...") as well as much more. Annoying contracts can also be renegotiated in a more satisfactory way ("But I always imagined you liked doing that!").

Best of all, by reviewing contracts we stay in the present with each other. We adjust to other changes in our lives, external and internal, by dealing with things freshly from one moment to the next. This way relationships become more fresh and alive, roles are given a chance to expand and grow, and we move away from a position of obligation (I have to do it whether I feel like it or not, because I promised) into a position of responsibility (I'll do it because right now it's what I feel like doing).

Obligation is a duty programmed into us in the past which rapidly becomes stale. For example, it is my duty to help little old ladies to cross the road. But why? I don't know, it's just something I was told to do. But what if the little old lady is not grateful or doesn't even want to be helped across the road? If I am so determined to fulfill my duty, I might be offended. If, on the other hand, it comes from a spontaneous desire to help, I will be open to the unpredictable response.

Obligation is something that most of us feel to greater and lesser degrees. How much we let it guide our lives depends on us, but to the extent that we do things we really don't want to do, the divided feeling inside us becomes a burden and eventually tires us out.

■ PARTS TO PLAY

Role playing is a means of gaining valuable insight into the dynamics of relationship. By consciously agreeing to play roles we eventually come to a

Never too young to start. Never too old to learn.

point where we are able to move more easily towards becoming masters of our roles rather than slaves to them. We increase the chance of getting what we need in our lives. Just as important, we come to understand just what it is that we do need.

Roles are something we play most of the time. Mother, wife, student, teacher, leader or follower, friend or enemy – some roles become more and more prevalent in time, giving less of a chance for others to be played out. For example, the mother takes care of her children for twenty-four hours a day. She may feel fulfilled by it, and yet something

seems to be missing. Deep inside she longs to be taken care of herself sometimes. She wants to be a child herself and be nurtured, but she is so busy that the urge doesn't have an opportunity for fulfillment. Unconscious resentment can grow from this. Without even knowing where the resentment comes from she may find it getting in the way of giving the support her kids and her husband may need. One evening she and her mate decide to do an experiment. For one evening she becomes the child and he becomes the father. His role is to take care of her and hers is to be nurtured. He prepares the food she loves, gives her a

bath, reads her a story. He does for her the things her real father used to do, or those things she would have liked him to have done but never did.

This is an example of role playing. The next night they switch roles. The powerful executive gets to be a little boy again. There are many possibilities to this exchange of roles, all it takes is memory and imagination.

Other roles could include: first date, strangers meeting for the first time, boyfriend and girl-friend, enemies, old folk, and even sex reversal where the woman plays the man and the man plays the woman.

The roles have physical postures, feelings and language associated with them. As we get familiar with these postures during the exercise, we learn to recognize parts of ourselves that are calling out for attention. We learn to respond to these calls. As a result, we become more clear on what we need. And when you know that, it is easier to ask for it and get it in day-to-day life.

DO IT YOURSELF

Having experimented with the exercises presented in the book, begin to create your own techniques. This can happen any time and anywhere. Once you have a feel for the types of things that work best for you, and that you enjoy doing the most, it becomes easy for you to create new ways of doing, relating and being in the world. Of course, you will have reservations, thinking you need to be an expert and to have devoted years of time to it – and there is some truth to this. At least until you slightly shift your viewpoint: you are an expert on yourself, you have been learning about yourself all your life. It is possible to put all this experience to good use.

By observing yourself more closely and factually, without resorting to judgment and criticism, you will be surprised to notice new and creative experiments popping up all the time. It takes a bit of curiosity and a willingness to experiment and to make mistakes.

Everything, from acupuncture and yoga through to the wheel and the light bulb, was invented by someone and developed over a period of time. People used their powers of observation and a bit of creativity to help new ideas come through.

You can do the same. Start in any area where you have experience and some interest. Whether in the shower, at work, watching TV or relating to friends, clients or kids, there are always areas you know a lot about. It does not matter how trivial you may think it is. Whatever works for you is right.

We stole, adapted and created our exercises over years of doing and teaching body-work and movement awareness. However, when we decided

Once you are in the swing of it let your intuition guide you.

to write this book, we realized that most techniques had to be adapted to different mediums – words and pictures. Up until this time we could present the exercise in person and correct any mistakes and answer any questions that might arise, on the spot. In a book this is not possible. Exercises have to be clear and uncomplicated leaving no room for misunderstanding. We had to re-work exercises as well as create new ones. We also had to anticipate questions and problems. In the course of doing this, we actually learned a lot of new ways of doing things ourselves. It is a never-ending process, a journey of discovery and delight. Once we were in the swing of it, the possibilities became endless. We invite you to join in the fun. To become an authority on yourself, you'll become an authority on living in balance!

■ EXPOSE YOURSELF

During the exercise of role-playing in *Parts to Play*, we explored the many uses different roles have in making us a more complete person. We looked at how we can consciously choose to be in certain roles and to move from one role to another. Through this process of exposing ourselves we can begin to expand the boundaries of our roles. We can build new bridges, new ways of contacting our fellow human beings.

Normally we keep certain sides of ourselves hidden from others, and often even from ourselves. Sometimes in times of great adversity, during wars and natural calamities, people share themselves more totally and generously than in daily life. Great acts of courage, compassion and personal sacrifice emerge.

But why wait for a war in order to expose your potential? Why not create special situations where it can happen by itself? Certainly there is some risk involved. What you reveal may not feel important enough, and people may laugh or judge or change their opinion of you. There is that chance, but life is sometimes a risky business, and some risk is both exhilarating and liberating. Furthermore, when we expose ourselves, especially to someone close to us, we are getting rid of the walls of protection that usually separate people. We come closer together; we share on a deeper level; we are more real. And reality is filled with love and acceptance. Except perhaps in certain British circles, the act of sharing and exposing oneself is usually greeted with respect and admiration by others. Try it and see for yourself.

Create a situation where you have some time to spend undisturbed with someone who is close to you. Pick some aspect of yourself that you have not, as yet, shared with them. It may be your vulnerability, or just as easily your strength – we keep some strange things hidden. It may be your aggressive side or your passive side, or your humor or your serious side. Tell intimate stories from your past to illustrate your point. Get into the feeling you are trying to express. Live it in that moment.

Begin easily; there is no need to jump right away into your darkest secrets. As the energy starts to build and flow you will get more confident. Do not show any side because you think that you must. Expose what you feel like. But be ready to take some risk if it feels right. After a while the exercise runs on its own steam, and there is no need to follow any structure. It is important, however, to give the other person a chance to also expose some part of himself to you, if he feels to. This makes the exercise more balanced and more fun. But do not force the other to do something that he does not want to do.

Once you have done this technique a few times you will find yourself sharing and exposing yourself more readily in your day-to-day life. No need to make a big deal out of it. You will be benefiting from its effects yourself, and it may or may not rub off on other people. Some people will enjoy and respond to it more than others. Some situations will be more conducive than others to this way of being. You will naturally seek out these kinds of situations in order to be able to relate in this way.

Many people still associate exposing oneself to dirty old men in raincoats. This is the fault of a society that tries to substitute conventions and rules of conduct for true feeling. Society is changing; it has to in order to survive in this crazy age. By changing our own attitudes, broadening our own horizons, we are assisting in raising the consciousness of the whole of the world around us.

■ FULL CIRCLE

This is a powerful and revealing exercise in relating. It brings new life and fresh blood to a relationship. It clears the air between people, making room for new and deeper levels of communication to take place. Whenever we spend a lot of time with someone it is inevitable that we fall into certain patterns. This prohibits us from being fully alive

1 Express your resentments.

2 Voice your appreciations.

3 Ask for and receive forgiveness.

with each other. This exercise is a fresh start, another good way to practice assertiveness, and it is a great way to accept others and ourselves in all the imperfections, idiosyncrasies and frailties that make us truly human.

The quality that comes through during the course of doing this technique is love. Love makes communication, understanding and acceptance possible. It enables us to be open and frank with each other. It allows room for forgiveness. Even if your heart does not feel open when you start this exercise, begin anyway. You will be pleasantly surprised that in sharing with another, the heart springs open of itself. Sometimes we pollute the atmosphere with all our petty problems, and, in this polluted atmosphere, the heart flower remains closed. Still it is there and ready to bloom at a moment's notice if we simply blow away the polluting air. Here is your chance.

Sit facing your partner so it is easy to have eye contact.

You start off by saying whatever comes into your mind that you resent about the other person. It can be anything and everything, silly or serious, minor or major, significant or petty. "I resent the way you squeeze the toothpaste in the middle of the tube... and I resent your sleepiness in general, especially because I feel I have to tidy up after you... and other people think you are tidy and it is really me... and people like you better then they like me... and I resent that you like to have so much fun, even when I am in a grumpy mood..."

This goes on for about five minutes, or until it feels like everything has been said that needs to be said. It may be difficult to begin, but, once the flow begins, it is easy and it feels good. Meanwhile, the other person just listens and takes in the information. Even if he feels provoked, or unjustly accused or whatever, it is essential that he does not respond in any way, neither with words nor facial expression.

Then, after a moment's pause, the roles are reversed. Resentments are expressed in the other direction.

When the resentment stage is complete, move on to the appreciation stage. "I appreciate your hair, the way you look, your smile, the way you are with the children... I appreciate the way you like to have fun even when I am grumpy – it cheers me up!"

Appreciations come easier after the resentments are out of the way. Often, resentments turn into appreciations once they are expressed and verbalized. We do not judge or defend or react in any way to either phase. Just take it in and with your body language encourage the other to go on pouring it out. Keep your body open, available and attentive to the person talking.

Be as total as possible in expressing both sides, without putting malice into your voice. Just report what you are feeling without getting hung up on any one point. By all means, emphasize anything you wish to, but the idea is to state as much and as many different aspects as you can.

The third part of the exercise is to take turns asking forgiveness of the other. A simple, "Can you forgive me for forgetting to call you the other night?" is all that is necessary. "Yes," is all the answer we need give. To ask for forgiveness, and to grant it, are both equally uplifting experiences. Once resentments and appreciations are aired it is so much easier to ask and to get forgiveness. For in the spirit of true sharing and openness there is hardly anything that needs to be forgiven.

AWAKENING

Being awake and aware is central to living in balance. Read this section slowly and carefully.

Awareness is the now. It is a state that is always available to us if we choose to take notice of it. Awareness is a state of expansion, an opening, a broadening of horizons. In contrast to this is the state of contraction. This is where the world seems either to be closing in on us or to be very far away, at the end of a long tunnel. In this state we are in a dream, moving, breathing, thinking, and relating as if it is not really us doing it. As if it is all a mechanical activity and we are robots, triggered into action by momentary whims of life that are sometimes benevolent, sometimes malevolent, and very often out of our control.

Awareness does not bring the things of your life under greater control or security; nor in fact does it act directly upon what you do. It alters nothing in itself. Yet its effect upon your life is profound and all-encompassing.

Right now as you read these words let yourself become more aware. Begin by noticing your eyes moving across the page. Awareness is the noticing. A moment before your eyes were moving across the page mechanically, unconsciously, doing something that they can do quite automatically without any problem. Yet as you bring an element of awareness into the picture things start to change

Like and arrow moving toward the target.

somewhat. If your eyes were straining unnecessarily you would become aware of this and spontaneously begin to relax them or to move into an area of better light, more suitable for reading. Normally we would only do this when the eyes become over-strained and hurt. The pain would cause us to act. But why wait until the damage has been done when by being a little more aware problems are automatically solved?

Feel now the way your hands hold the book, including the actual grip of the fingers. Notice the angle of the wrists and of the elbows. More than likely as you notice these minute details a slight re-arrangement begins to occur. The fingers may relax a bit, the elbows or wrists change their direction a bit, and you get a little more comfortable. This happens without thinking about it or even trying to change. The body when given the choice chooses the most relaxed way of being.

Pay a little attention to your shoulders now. Are they up or down, hunched or relaxed. How about the head? What's happening there? Is it sitting in comfortable balance or are the muscles having to

work overtime? Check your jaws: clenched or free?

We now have a circle of awareness starting from the eyes, going through the shoulders, arms and hands and back up to the head and eyes. See if you can feel that full circle and then include the breath into it. Breath is movement, change – the flow of life. When the breath is moving fully and freely and we are in an aware state we open ourselves up to the fullness of life around and within us. We are able to adapt to the changing demands of each moment because we are in the present moment. We are aware.

Awareness does not act. We act. Awareness makes it possible to act in a more expansive way. It gives us more choices. It is as if we are groping around in a dark room and suddenly the light is turned on. Awareness is that light. It makes life much easier and more enjoyable.

Now broaden the focus of your awareness to include the whole of your body. Feel the parts that are making contact with the chair. See if you can feel your skin making contact with your clothing, even making contact with the air around you.

Awareness is in the body, mind, and feelings. It is everywhere. We are awareness itself. Yet we can live without awareness, but it is a sleepy and habitual life, lived in a dark and gray world.

In the process of becoming more aware it is easiest to start with the body. This is the focus of the book. As we become more conscious of our bodies it is then easier to include the mind, noticing the processes constantly happening there. Awareness is not a mind process at all. It is a wakefulness that includes the mind but goes far beyond it.

Athletes identify with their bodies, intellectuals with their minds, while emotions are felt most when we are in a feminine, receptive state. We are the body, we are the mind, we are the feelings, but we are also much more. We are awareness (see diagram).

You may be angry and not know it. The anger builds. Suddenly you blow your top and kick the dog or shout at your child. Or perhaps the anger manifests as a coolness to your loved-one. You have no idea why you are so cool and spiteful, just that it's happening and you cannot help yourself.

Enter awareness. You notice your coolness. You see that it has nothing to do with the other person. You tell them this, asking them to be patient until the mood passes. You reflect back over the day and remember the episode that triggered your anger. You realize it was not even so much the episode itself that caused such a strong and lingering reaction, only that it reminded you of some trauma in your early life. A light has been shed upon the darkness of your inner being, and with the help of this light you are able to start fresh, returning to the reality of the moment.

Furthermore, had the awareness been present earlier in the day when the event that got you angry happened, your response would have been different. Unaware people react. Their reaction is predictable, pre-programmed, and narrow. Awareness responds. In the moment it seeks to act in a fresh and appropriate way, in keeping with the real nature of the situation.

Perhaps you would have become angry in that moment and by releasing the anger not have allowed it to grow and become warped. Or you might have understood the nature of your feeling then and there, seen where it came from in the past, and through understanding, changed the anger into simply a lesson to be learned in life. We cannot predict what the aware person will do because their response is unique to the moment. It comes out of clarity rather than darkness. It is enlightened.

Awareness is the single most powerful tool of transformation available to us. The other great tool is love; love for ourselves, for our friends, for humanity, and for the whole of creation. Love truly does make the world go around. And awareness is the sun that provides the light that permits us to see the wonder of this world.

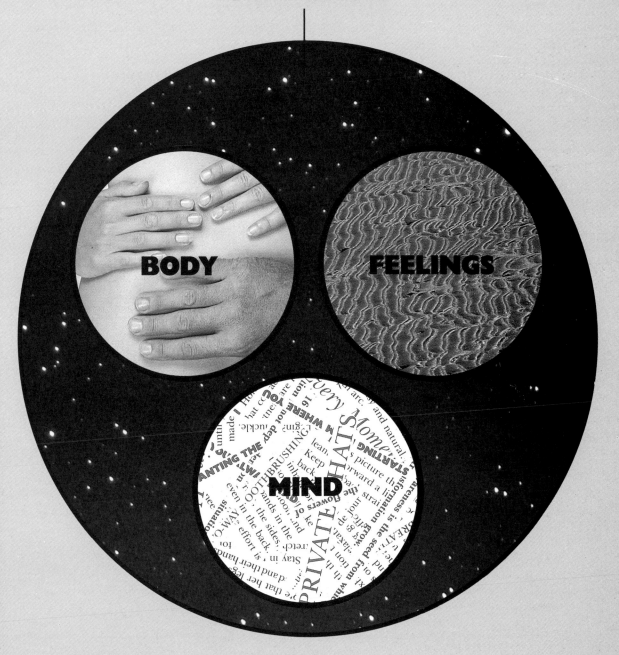

CELEBRATE EVERYTHING

Life is not always an easy affair. There are wars, famines, diseases, and calamities galore both man-made and natural. Over 200,000 people die every day, well over a million a week. And death is only the beginning of our problems. In the city of Bombay alone there are over four million homeless people sleeping on the street, in makeshift huts or out in the open.

These kinds of statistics from all over the world could fill pages and pages of this book. But even those of us who are lucky enough not to be a statistic at this moment have our problems. We who in the eyes of society have achieved some degree of success are left with an uneasy feeling: now what? Do we pursue more success and riches; do we try for more security, more excitement, more distraction? Do we look for solace in the religions, in the arts, in our families, in charitable actions, in fantasy, in sex, in power, in inner growth? Just what direction do we move in, and is it really worth moving in any direction at all?

If you are looking for the answers to these questions in this book you will be disappointed. We don't know the answers any more than you do. And even if we did and were to tell you, it would possibly be the cruelest thing we could do. The mysteries of existence handed over on a plate would probably make life unbearably dull. For one thing does seem clear: this life of ours is a mysterious affair. It is a kind of school to which we have all come to learn certain lessons. Many of the lessons are similar to each other, and many of the situations we go through are the same again and again.

But the way we respond and the combinations of situations that arise for each one of us will mold us in a certain way that is individual and uniquely ours.

Many great scientists have stated that the more deeply they fathom the mysteries of their chosen field, the more brand-new mysterious things pop up. The mystics say much the same thing. They have explored the mysteries of their inner beings with a rare totality. Some have reached great plateaus of contentment and bliss. And yet they report that the mystery has no end. In fact, life just seems to get more and more magical. Each moment is an unexpected happening, another chance to explore another new mystery.

If this is true and life really is an endless exploration, it implies several things. One is that there is no end in itself that will provide us with perfect happiness and contentment and an ending to the learning process. This makes it impossible to look into the future for some development that will change everything: if only I could win the lottery, or find true love, or fathom the secrets of the universe, then everything will be all right. It does not seem to work that way. This is, however, not to say that we should not seek love, fulfillment, happiness or whatever matters to us. It is more to suggest that within the very search itself we will discover what we are seeking.

Or perhaps it is the way in which we seek, the very fabric of our lives, that is important. Maybe it is not the end that is important at all, but the means by which we move towards that end. All the mystics talk about the present moment, right now, right here. That is where it is all happening. Sounds like a nice idea but one that is hard to live. Crammed like sardines into a subway train, suffocating from lack of air, who wants to be here and now? Let me be anywhere else but in the moment.

Having said that, the fact remains that while we are on the subway train, we are on the subway train. It is at this point that we are left with a rather momentous decision: do we do the seemingly obvious thing and suffer through the ride until we reach our destination. Or do we celebrate?

Celebrate what? When this situation is so terrible? Well, that too is something. We can celebrate the terribleness of the moment. The absolute bottom line is: it's all that's happening right now, so why not make the most of it!

Life has its ups and downs, its good days and its bad days. It manifests like two sides of one coin, constantly flipping.

But it appears that both are necessary in order for us to learn all the lessons that we are meant to learn. So why not celebrate the bad along with the good? We have all had days when all of our plans have gone so wrong, all our hopes shattered, and we are on the point of despair. And then when it seems like nothing more can go wrong, something else does. And to our great surprise, instead of

committing suicide right there on the spot, we start laughing, a full, deep and thoroughly enjoyable belly laugh. We laugh for no particular reason except at the whole ridiculous nature of our lives

The situation need not affect the celebration.

at that moment. And in that moment our whole focus has changed. We are celebrating. Everything that was wrong remains wrong, and yet we are no longer so involved, so it does not seem so serious and devastating. The very fact of being alive seems to bring us enough pleasure.

This is what we mean by celebrating. And it does seem that we have the choice in each and every moment of our lives to celebrate or not to celebrate. We can celebrate joy and we can celebrate anger. We can celebrate love and we can celebrate heartache. We are still experiencing whatever it is that we are experiencing – that has not changed. What has changed is the place from which we are viewing things. If life really is a school, maybe this is a very significant lesson we are in the middle of learning. And who knows what the lesson is leading on to? If we are too busy feeling sorry for our misfortune, we may miss the very lesson life is trying to show us and have to repeat the situation over and over again until we get it.

And if as the mystics say, "life is a mystery to be lived, not a problem to be solved," then we might as well celebrate right now this particular mystery and await the next one.

Celebration is a subtle shift in orientation. If we see that when something has gone wrong, we are not being punished by life but rather it is just the way it is sometimes, then we celebrate. And when we are in a mode of celebration we are more open to what is truly occurring in that moment and to what is to come.

Rengetsu was a female mystic in the Zen tradition. While traveling on a pilgrimage she arrived at a village just before nightfall. She went to the villagers, asking for lodging for the night but was refused by everyone. She was forced to spend the night outside under the stars. She was awakened in the middle of the night by the cold. In the light of the full moon she saw the fully opened cherry blossoms. So overcome by their beauty, she wrote this poem:

Through their kindness
in refusing me lodging
I found myself beneath the blossoms
on the night of this misty moon.

This poem reflects an attitude of celebration. Had Rengetsu been moping and feeling sorry for herself she could not have enjoyed the beauty of the night, nor ever been able to forgive, let alone thank, those who turned her away. Life must have revealed one of its mysteries to this unique woman and she was in the right attitude to be able to appreciate the lesson. She was celebrating.

Begin by really celebrating joyful occasions to their fullest. Then let yourself celebrate ordinary things: a sunset, the wind in the trees, the sound of laughter, a good joke. Then let your mood carry over into everyday life. Washing the car, stuck in a traffic jam, turn everyday activity, even frustrations and aggravations, into celebration. Finally, let yourself experience the so-called bad

Gratefulness.

things that happen to you. Do not run from them; don't feel overly sorry for yourself; try celebration. Of course you will often forget and find yourself running away, or otherwise giving yourself a hard time. When you finally notice yourself doing it, celebrate that too. If you cry, if you feel pain deeply and totally, if you are overwhelmed by occurrences, if you are angry and hateful – celebrate it. It just means you are alive and participating in life's lessons. It can't make things worse, but it does have the capacity to make things better.

ACKNOWLEDGMENTS

Martin Adam: 72, 73

BBC HULTON LIBRARY: 12, 44, 52, 53, 204

THE BRIDGEMAN ART LIBRARY: 161, 167

BRITISH MUSEUM: 51, 197

Loriano Fanara: 98

Mark Greenberg: 203

HUTCHINSON LIBRARY: 19, 199

THE IMAGE BANK: 88

IMAGES COLOR LIBRARY: 27

K & B NEWS FOTO – Aldo Zaccagna: 7
Massimo Guadagni: 65
F. Bartolini: 137
M. Guarducci: 146
S. Cellai: 198
G. Garrasi: 147
G. Oliva: 58

MARY EVANS PICTURE LIBRARY: 164

UNIVERSAL STUDIO: 176, 177

Oriano Rontini: 99

SCIENCE PHOTO LIBRARY – Alexander Tsiaras: 56

SYNDICATION INTERNATIONAL Ltd.: 54, 89

SUSAN GRIGGS AGENCY: 28, 95, 96, 110, 135